SPIRITED CLEARINGS

Negative Program Removal

DR. MARGARET (MEG) HOOPES & ELI GALLA

BALBOA.
PRESS

A DIVISION OF HAY HOUSE

Balboa Press books may be ordered through booksellers or by contacting:

Balboa Press
A Division of Hay House
1663 Liberty Drive
Bloomington, IN 47403
www.balboapress.com
1-(877) 407-4847

ISBN: 978-1-4525-4412-0 (sc)
ISBN: 978-1-4525-4411-3 (hc)
ISBN: 978-1-4525-4410-6 (e)

Library of Congress Control Number: 2011963016

Because of the dynamic nature of the Internet, any web addresses or links contained in this book may have changed since publication and may no longer be valid. The views expressed in this work are solely those of the author and do not necessarily reflect the views of the publisher, and the publisher hereby disclaims any responsibility for them.

The author of this book does not dispense medical advice or prescribe the use of any technique as a form of treatment for physical, emotional, or medical problems without the advice of a physician, either directly or indirectly. The intent of the author is only to offer information of a general nature to help you in your quest for emotional and spiritual well-being. In the event you use any of the information in this book for yourself, which is your constitutional right, the author and the publisher assume no responsibility for your actions.

Any people depicted in stock imagery provided by Thinkstock are models, and such images are being used for illustrative purposes only.
Certain stock imagery © Thinkstock.

Printed in the United States of America

Balboa Press rev. date: 2/22/2012

Contents

Foreword: Eli's Introduction

Meg started this manual about a year or so before she transitioned. Shortly before she died, she gave permission to the women of Ashtar on the Road to take on her work and finish it. They asked me to edit it, calling upon the insights and kind help of my teaching partner Katharina, and Meg's friends Leslie and Iris.

The members of the Ashtar on the Road team, Susan, Elise, and Fran, have provided help in rounding up a lot of Meg's material as well as making available the insights of Ashtar and Mother Sekhmet.

Meg was a very energetic, vital, and dynamic woman who taught school from grade 5 through graduate studies. She did energy work and clearings for a very long time. Her intuition and her curious nature served her well. It was with the support of Ashtar that she started her own conference calls in 2009. She served us by teaching us how to do the clearings on our own and how to disseminate them to others.

The thing that attracted me to Meg's teachings was that she presented the most effective way I have ever experienced to remove the negative programs. I had been studying ways of getting rid of these fear-based programs and how to re-imprint with higher vibrations for over thirty years. Meg made it easy and taught us that we could rely on our own intuition and use muscle response testing, pendulums, or our inner knowing to find answers to our questions, and she said that we have the help of the angelic beings and ascended masters if we use the power of intent.

These clearings free a person into enabling their own process upon the ascension path. The clearing and transmutation of the energy that held this negative programming in place enables the person to be ascension ready.

I had used Muscle Response Testing with other healing modalities before, but Meg got me into using it not just for facilitating sessions on myself and others. When I used MRT with her removals, I saw very positive results. I realized the more I used it, the more I would get into my heart and access my intuition. The questions I asked when I did MRT reflected my level of trust with my connection to spirit. I would be guided to ask questions that were in alignment with getting to the heart of my concerns, and the answers would come.

I feel it is important to note that when we are working in sessions with individuals, we can remove the root causes of the person's separation from spirit. We can ask questions with Muscle Response Testing, pendulums, or our own inner knowing that will tell us what negative programs or negative entities are still active. We ask in what lifetime this program or entity originated, because this originating lifetime is our starting point. We clear all of the lifetimes, timelines, and aspects of ourselves from this starting point.

Time has passed since Meg had the inspiration to do these clearings, and we are further into the ascension process. It is now necessary to accomplish more in a given amount of time, so we have to use our intuition more. At the same time the light is much more dominant. It is up to us to take this into account, so people will be able to hold their own attitudes of trusting their intuition and self-perception in a faster mode than even three years ago. Trust and testing go together.

Mother Sekhmet has told us that it will help to have a smoother flow to a session if we take about five minutes to connect with the higher self of the person with whom we will be doing the session, before the person comes on the phone or starts a session with us in person. Doing this type of pre-session gives us more information about the client.

You can speak to the person's higher self and ask, "How strong is this person's trust?" You could say, "Joe is coming in half an hour. Before I meet with Joe, I want to prepare for a session that will give him maximum benefits and help him absorb and assimilate as much of the light that will come into his being from releasing negative programs."

You can ask any questions you want to about Joe, but one of the key ones is: "What is Joe's level of trust in the processes we will be using? How open is he to this facilitation?" Not because you're going to be dismayed if it's a three on a scale of ten, but it's simply for your own knowing, because maybe the first thing you have to do is introduce Joe to the unseen helpers who are going to be there and ask him to feel the energies. Maybe you want to do just a slight preparation, where Joe can lift up to where he can get his trust levels higher.

So you say, "I choose to speak to Joe's subconscious. Am I speaking with Joe's subconscious, yes or no?" You muscle test for the answer. If the answer is yes, you say, "I choose to know about Joe's level of trust for this procedure we are about to embark on together. On a scale of zero to ten, where is Joe's trust? Is it less or more than five?" Then you go in the direction of less or more until you come up with the exact number.

You're not going to find a lot of people with ten, especially if they are coming for their first time, because they don't know you. They haven't been through the procedures, except for maybe what they've read on Meg's website, and that is a lot different than if they come on the phone; the same is just as true when they come in person. Establish the level of trust, and if it's below five, it would be most advantageous to work consciously with Joe for the first two to five minutes of your time together, to get the trust level up. You want to bring in the angels and the ascended masters and have Joe feel his divine nature, because what you do with Joe from then on will be a lot more successful.

What you really want to do is touch upon where they are living; this means you want to connect with the different aspects of their being. The reason we use the different aspects of their being is because quite often they're going to come in with the ego doing a little tap dance. They're coming into the session not knowing you and not knowing exactly what to expect. They're going to have a little bit of ego pulling on them. You can ask to speak to their subconscious, their higher self, and to all of their guidance team. Don't stop with the individual—get them to open to these other aspects of their being.

But remember, if the person's trust level is low, the objective is to elevate them up and out of those three lower chakra areas of concentration, particularly number three, where the ego is speeding it up for them. That is something you can do for them, before you engage with them to a certain extent, but you can also incorporate working with them to elevate. You can utilize some of the things you already know, and you can put together a very simple procedure.

In this day and age expansion doesn't take much. It can turn on like a water faucet, this feeling of elevation, of getting in touch with the higher energies. With a lot of people you just say a sentence or two, and they feel it. Why? Because you've gone into those energies for them to partake of, and all you're really doing is asking them to reach out and allow the energies to come into their fields on a more conscious level. Beam love and let them feel that for a moment.

Say to yourself, "I am the facilitator." It starts with the teacher setting the stage. Some of the people we will work with don't have a clue of what their role is. You only need two to five minutes to call in all of the pieces of Joe and yourself that are interdimensional. You inquire about Joe's level of trust, and then you set the tone for the session by doing this pre-session with the higher self & its teams.

When you are doing this pre-session, you might want to connect with Meg on a direct basis. You can offer an invitation for Meg to take a permanent seat on your own council of guidance. You can offer an introduction of who you are, what your intent in doing this work is, and then invite Meg into the group of guidance. This will allow Meg to further her service through you.

In this manual, with the help of the woman of Ashtar on the Road, Meg's friends, and Mother Sekhmet and Ashtar, I have attempted to present as much info about Meg's teachings and insights into the spirited clearings as I could. Sometimes there is information in the form of stories about these clearings, so I have included some of that as well.

I feel it is important to remember that all of these clearings are done with us connected with spirit in our heart centers. Love is the highest vibrational healing tool we have. We are all divine sovereign beings; these clearings help us empower ourselves by regaining our natural integrity.

Who Is Meg Hoopes?

Written by Dr. Margaret (Meg) Hoopes

It has been suggested that I describe how I developed myself and how I discovered and evolved the spirited clearings that I teach. I was born in Idaho Falls, Idaho on May 12, 1927, to loving parents and a large extended family; I was the second child of five. We lived in a rural area at a time when the nation was recovering from World War I and the financial depression that followed it. Everyone worked hard and managed to have some fun doing it. Social activities revolved around the church, worship services, funerals, school events, bazaars, dances, plays, and programs. Everyone in our family loved to read. With no community library, no TV, and few newspapers, we relied on trading reading materials and the radio.

From those early experiences, I learned how to work without complaint, to finish what I started and do it well, to work with others, to appreciate family and friends and the community, to tell the truth, and to learn by observing others. When I was three years old, I told my mother I would be a teacher. In spite of many difficult hurdles, I never wavered from that goal. I completed a BS in education, with a minor in physical education and a major in English. I was certified to teach fifth to twelfth grades, and I taught in all of them. I was also a school counselor for girls. I had a psychology class, but I believe I learned more about human behavior by observing others and puzzling about my own behavior and motives. Curiosity led to many discoveries.

I perceived the degrees which I received in the field of education as union cards that allowed me to do what I was interested in doing and getting paid for it. I eventually received an MS in personnel and guidance. Later, I went to the University of Minnesota and received a PhD in counseling psychology, which allowed me to teach graduate classes and supervise graduate students in school counseling and marriage and family therapy. Through all of those experiences, I was observing and asking questions of my teachers, my fellow students, and my spirit. It became my experience that very few theories of behavior—and how to change behaviors, emotions, and beliefs—included love and spiritual sources. The scientific method prevailed: "If you can't see it, touch it, smell it, hear it, and measure it, it does not exist."

When I was teaching or doing therapy, I often said or did appropriate things, but I had no conscious recollection of where they came from. I sensed and felt things that I had no rational explanation for how I received this information. I began to study the energy of the body, going outside of the box I had lived in, and I found a wealth of information. I went to workshops and weekend programs, such as Lifespring1*.

I suddenly became aware of books that took me far out of my box. I facilitated weekend growth retreats, constantly learning, stretching, inviting, and experiencing miracles. I saw a few psychics and learned about their lifetimes. I received information from the beings in the unseen world. Channeled information intrigued me and led me to new experiences of the unseen world. All of this led me to a greater knowingness. As a child I learned that there were angels, that I had a spirit that lived within me, and that there was life after death. I learned more about those events and the many dimensions of energy. I read, and I attended a variety of classes such as the cosmic energy classes, with emphasis on laser Reiki, the Ramtha School of Enlightenment, the St Germaine Sanctuary, and many others. (See the glossary of terms, Appendix E, at the back of book.)

All of the clearings on my website were inspired by my experiences and information downloaded from ascended masters and lady masters, galactics, angels, archangels, and my "I Am" presence. My curiosity led me to my wonder chair, where I wondered in the early hours of the day from 3:30 to 4:30 a.m., and was given answers to my questions that sprang forth from my curiosity.

To read more about the wonder process and its results, go to my website and read the story of the disrupter. The disrupter was removed from the planet by a ceremony conducted by the whammy group with the assistance of three trillion light workers, cosmic beings, and all who serve the planet at this time. Each one of the clearings has its own story of evolution and uses. My experiences with Ashtar and the Ashtar group led me to having a website built for me, teaching the dendrite removals, and doing conference calls.

I am filled with wonder, love, joy, and a fountain of spontaneous laughter. People ask me what I am laughing about, because I am the only one laughing. It is as though I have a cosmic knowledge that pleases me so much, and the laughter bubbles out of me. There is a sacred feather within that tickles me, and I revel in the joy and happiness I feel. It happens when I am alone and when I am with others; it is not secret. I know it is sacred! The sureness of that knowingness fills me with wonder. Perhaps that part of me that knows the alpha and omega of our journeys with Mother Gaia joyously laughs every time one more of us awakens to the knowledge of who we are, awakens to our light shining brighter and brighter, awakens to the love surrounding us and filling us. We are responding to the sure knowledge that our days of slavery and servitude to those whom we do not want controlling us are over.

Several years ago a friend gave me a T-shirt with these words printed on it: "Expect a Miracle." All miracles are fueled with love and intention. I am amazed at the multitude of miracles in my life and those around me. I am so grateful for the miracle of the clearings and methods granted me through divine guidance for releasing negative dendrites, memories, and habits, for cleansing and purifying our lives. I honor and love you for the miracle of acceptance by you who have chosen to do your housecleaning using these methods and the clearings that bless Mother Gaia and all of us. We are One!

When I teach a class or have sessions with individuals, I am both the teacher and learner. You who participate are both the learner and the teacher. Miracles happen in that exchange, and we pass those miracles on in how we conduct and share our lives. This happens every day and sometimes many times in the same day. My fountain of spontaneous laughter is a miracle and is continually fed by miracles.

To the readers of this manual, I send you blessings and love so that you may acknowledge, claim, and enjoy your fountain of spontaneous laughter.

PART ONE

CHAPTER 1

Expansion 101:
Calling on Our Teams and Angels

When we are dreaming in a heavy sleep state, we go back to the other side of this life. This is the place from which we started our journey of being a human in this lifetime; it is there that we access the interdimensional aspects of our being, and this is the time we are the most expansive. This is the place that many of us call Home, and it is the place we return to before we start our next journey as an incarnated being.

Before we go to sleep, we can make a focus using our breathing. It is with our breathing that we slow down, connect from our heart center to Creator-Source, and bring in the higher frequencies being beamed to us from the central sun. We can ask for our guidance and angel teams to give us divine protection, both while we are awake doing our meditations and traveling all over creation and also while we are doing our sleeptime work. We can ask them to help us bypass the astral planes and to ensure that no lower dimensional beings or energies attach themselves to us.

It is quite beneficial to give our guidance teams and angels gratitude. When we are in a state of gratitude, we keep the gateways between us and the spirit open. Giving gratitude is a way to acknowledge that we chose to be here and are happy to be able to play our part in this divine dance of life.

We can call in our guidance before we go to sleep and after we wake up the next morning. We ask these unseen beings of light to keep us connected with Creator-Source. We ask them to help guide and inspire us throughout our day and night.

Giving yourself the intent to relax and let go with your breathing in a long, deep, slow fashion will enable you to bring in the higher frequencies of love and light, as well as strengthen the connection with your angels and guidance. You can do it basically anywhere, and it is helpful to keep your eyes closed, but it isn't necessary.

We are told by our mentors—Ashtar, Sananda, Mother Sekhmet, Mother Mary, Qwan Yin, St. Germaine, and our team of angels and guides, ascended masters, and other beings of light—that if we call them in, they will shine their light of love on us, and it will help us remember who we are and let us continue to feel the connection with Creator-Source when we are awake or in our sleeping state.

When we set our intention and allow ourselves to know it will work, it will. You can say, "Loving Sananda, with your gifts of unconditional love and forgiveness, please be with me today and help me retain memories of who I am. I ask you to prevent any astral beings from attaching themselves to me." Or you can say, "I ask and intend for the most benevolent outcomes." As soon as you say it, it is done. Gratitude is one of the surest ways that we stay connected with the Creator-Source. We cannot thank too much those unseen beings of light with which we co-create. Doubt and worry will limit the effects of what we are asking for.

Our angels and guides only want the best for us and are always with us. All we have to do is to say what we would like them to do, and it is done. All of the higher vibrations are expansive and pure. True love, unconditional and universal, is the highest vibrational healing tool in all of creation.

We are so much more than we have been taught to believe; who we are is beyond the limited structure of duality. We must learn to honor ourselves as interdependent, unlimited, divine, interdimensional, eternal beings of love and light. It is from this place of acknowledgment that we are here to fully expand our energy into that of Christed beings that we begin to accept we are here for a reason.

Each of us has unique gifts to manifest during our lives and share with all of creation. It is up to us to trust in the guidance we receive from our teams of angels and guides, whom we call in to help us carry out our plans for our journey through this lifetime.

Extending Ourselves into the Crystalline Grid

We are here on beloved Mother Gaia in this time of evolution. All of us came into this lifetime knowing that there was the opportunity to ascend to full consciousness while still being inside of a body. As I write this, that process for the planet and all beings on the planet is in full swing.

The upgrade from our cells being carbon based to being crystalline based is now approaching its apex. This transformation has been in process since the harmonic convergence in 1987. In this span of time, we have been learning how to balance the heart with the mind and body. We have been going through quite a challenging time as our brains have been rewired to hold these higher frequencies, which has caused us to expand our energy fields. All it takes is our conscious intent to lift ourselves up and raise the level of our vibrations, so that we can partake in the acceleration of these higher light frequencies coming into our planet's atmosphere.

Everything that isn't of the highest vibration will not function in the new earth that we have been building with the collective light of our love. It is up to us to continue to facilitate this acceleration of moving up in vibration, for the planet and us, to a light body. We do this by clearing the karmic residue of all the issues we have been working through during our many lifetimes on Mother Gaia.

Now is the time to do our housecleaning, as Ashtar has been saying for some time now. All of the issues we have been working on during this lifetime that haven't been healed are now coming up to be transmuted and raised to a higher level of consciousness. We can't stay in the higher dimensions while we have the lower vibrations around these issues attached to us.

Spirited clearings can be a vital part of this process. By clearing the negative programming attached to these issues, we allow ourselves to receive more of the higher light frequencies being beamed at us during this time of shift. Before we do the clearings, we call in the teams of angels and guides, which co-create with us, to help us to expand our energy. They are in mission with us to raise the level of consciousness for the All That Is.

Many of the higher light beings that are helping us are galactic beings. All of us on planet Earth are also of galactic origin. The higher light beings are helping us with our ascension. The rise into the higher dimensions is affected positively by us letting go of the negativity preventing us and Gaia from rising up. The galactics have a prime interest in seeing us evolve; they were responsible for designing our genetics and writing the codes to them inside our DNA.

The clearings will help you get back to a zero point. It took a lot of energy to hold the negative, fear-based programming in place. When we clear the negative programming the energy that has been transmuted is available to us to create from a place of unconditional, universal love. After we've done the clearings, our spiritual connection will be upgraded. This is where we extend our vibrations into the crystalline grid, which has been formed since the light became dominant on Gaia. Crystalline cities are being built, and this is indicative of us going back to unity consciousness, which is where we all came from before we started playing this game of being human on Gaia.

The clearings aren't about learning a specific process, doing it once in a while, and thinking you will get a quick fix from it. The clearings allow us to have dramatic lifestyle changes. This means it is up to us to make choices that will be in alignment with staying connected to the Creator-Source, expanding our consciousness by balancing the connection between our mind and body. This also means balancing the male and female energies inside of us, which you can think of as balancing the right and left lobes of your brain, or your emotional body with your mental body.

You can imagine that because of the negative programming and the karma that has resulted from it, we have been trapped in boxes of lower consciousness that benefitted those that controlled the money supply and resources of the planet. The clearings help us take back the energy stolen from us by mind control and many types of negative programming. It is up to us to find the pathways back into being centered in our hearts and continuously finding ways to bless and release anything that is not of the highest vibrations of love and light.

All of us must take back our bodies by allowing ourselves to connect our minds up with our hearts, so we can access the gifts we possess. The fear-based programming cut us off from being inside our bodies for so long, which has allowed the densest parts of duality to dominate our collective consciousness for thousands of years, since the last fall of Atlantis.

There are no limits to what you can create within the realm of using these clearings as a tool to accelerate ascension. When we clear the negative programming, we peel off another layer of the onion, as it were; this enables us to be more at the core of our essence and bring into the bodies of our being the love we all are.

Being Dendrite Sensitive

It will help us greatly to be what Meg called being dendrite sensitive. This means that we learn how to observe our thoughts and feelings. When we see and feel ourselves slide into an old pattern of not letting go and holding onto what doesn't feel good, we can train ourselves to observe the thoughts around these feelings. The energy becomes constricted, and the bodies of our being feel heavy. When we feel this we can muscle test and ask if there are negative programs, which negative dendrites are part of, active within us. We can also ask if handlers are active within us.

Not being in the "Now" moment, and finding it hard to open up to the wonder and possibilities of who we really are and why we came here, shows us that there is something blocking our energy. A heavy or uncomfortable feeling in the brain is a sign that some program or dendrite is sapping our energy and limiting our consciousness at some level. Some degree of fear is magnetizing us to lower vibrating thoughts.

We deliberately empower ourselves when we call in our guidance and connect into our heart center. You will find that the more layers of the negative programming you clear, the stronger the connection with Creator-Source becomes and the easier it is to stay connected.

When we go to the originating lifetime of a negative program and clear it, we gift ourselves with learning the message of why we created it. We ask questions of what it was like in that lifetime—what we did for a living, what our families were like, and what conflicts we had to deal with. It becomes possible for us to see the beauty of the journey we have been on, because we can develop a sense of compassion for all we have done to play out the polarities of the light against the dark.

The feeling of being in the state of universal, unconditional love is one of lightness, warmth, and expansion. You will feel you are in an effortless flow of energy. The opposite is being in a state of fear where we feel lack

& limitation, tightness, a sense of longing, and not being at peace. It triggers the mind into giving you an alert that something is wrong. The ego feeds off of the fear, and sometimes it seems like a long time before we are back in a balanced state once more.

It is up to us to raise the level of our vibration. We can do this by taking long, slow, deep breaths and calling in our guidance. We can remember anything that gives us joy and focus on a person, place, or thing we love. It is up to us to allow the song of freedom to play in our hearts, stop our minds from wandering, and focus on the love and light of the One we all are.

When we empower ourselves with unconditional, universal love, it is as if we are drinking from a limitless fountain of wonder, inspiration, and joy. It is ours for the asking; it is unlimited; it is our birthright; it is the truth of what and who we are. When our minds tell us we are less than this, they are lying to us. It is up to us to trust in the feeling of connection with Creator-Source. It is an expansive, unlimited place where the lower vibrations, all based in fear, cannot penetrate.

Fear is the most powerful weapon that the dark forces have to control us on this planet. When we expand the light of our love and focus it where there is little or no love, the power of their darkness evaporates. No fear can grow where there is love.

The more of us who get rid of the old programs, the faster we will all raise the level of consciousness so that these changes of moving into ascension can take place—not just for ourselves, but for the All That Is. Nothing and no one are separate. All of creation is connected to every other thing in a most beautiful and integral way.

Using Our Gifts

When we call in the energy of the beloveds from the other side, some of us are able to visualize being in the higher dimensions. Some of us picture ourselves among the angels and ascended masters, or we see ourselves flying around the multi-verse, and we are able to see planets and stars up close. Some of us can hear messages from beings of light; others are vibrational healers and feel the joy of who they are when they sing, dance, or play music. Some make movies, take photos, draw, or paint to inspire themselves and others; some love to write. At the root of our gifts is the connection to the Source. It is here in this reservoir of unlimited inspiration where we fill our cups and create our masterpieces.

Many of us have inspired and comforted people by being good listeners and good friends. We've always been there for our friends and have helped instill joy within them by caring about them, playing with them, and being a reflection of their energy by being in love with the living of our lives. We see and feel no separation between them and ourselves.

Most of us don't know the effect we have on others, but nonetheless we have affected others in a very positive way when we open our hearts and shine out our love to the rest of creation. We raise the level of our consciousness whenever we are in our passion; this simply means being and expressing our love. The level of our passion reflects how much we are in love with the living of our lives.

Some people are passionate about other people. Some are passionate about their animals and growing gardens full of luscious vegetables or beautiful flowers. Some are passionate about sports and inspire others to live up to their full potential, to be confident and not let fear rule their lives.

Every one of us who participates in our lives at a level of self-love and joy raises our own level of consciousness, which raises the level of consciousness for the All That Is. Love is the highest vibrational healing tool. Others can't help but feel good when we are so much in love with being here and playing this game of life with them. They may not even realize the effect you have on them, but they always come to you for advice, to hear your stories, to be with you and feel your energy. When we express our love, it raises the level of vibration for the All That Is. However we express our love, it is a gift to ourselves and to others.

When we do the clearings, I encourage everyone to observe how their gifts, particularly their intuitive gifts, are coming into play, and I ask you to give intent to receive information about how to better utilize them. For instance, when we go to the original lifetime to clear a program, we may have vivid imagery come up of what that lifetime was like for us: what our role was, what we did for a livelihood in that lifetime, what the environment was like, who was in our family, et cetera. Sometimes we may hear information that will help us, or the person we are working with, to clear negative programs or fears.

Being Consistently Connected to the One

Doing the dreamtime work with your guides and angels, as well as intergalactic teams on the ships, will help you expand your consciousness. By asking for this gateway to the other side to stay open, there is less chance for the handlers to attach themselves to you and infect you with negative dendrites and negative programs. Also, the more you use your tools—meditation, the power of intent, and imagination—and these clearings, the more sensitive you're going to be when the repetitive, lower vibrational thoughts come up that indicate you have negative programming or handlers active within you. After a while you are going to find that any time negative thoughts start to come in and jabber in your mind, you're going to be able to feel them, and it will be easier for you to observe them and let them go.

The emotions that are based in fear won't be able to take you over like they once did. You can simply say no and release them; you don't have to go for the emotional attachment and drama that surrounds them. Almost immediately you will see they are based in fear and that the more you buy into them, the less connected to Creator-Source you are going to be. You will come to see that these negative thoughts and emotions that don't feel good will no longer serve you, so they will fall away from your being. You will feel that the same old programming no longer magnetizes you to its vibration; it will now be easy for you to let go of the old patterns.

Whenever you feel that negativity is trying to come in and run your mind and emotions, you can call in your guidance teams of angels and ascended masters. Allowing their energy to come in helps you to be more into the Now moment. It is in this now moment that you can create what you desire. When you let go in the now moment, it is also called going to the zero point.

You are an integral part of the whole. Your thoughts, words, and actions can raise the level of vibration for All That Is. Allow yourself to feel the joy and love you are. Your energy expands when you focus on your love and light; in this way you strengthen your connection to Creator-Source.

The Ascension Lifestyle

It is important for us as students of the ascension process to know that our angels and guides want us to succeed, and that they will do everything they are allowed to do by the laws of the universe and the divine decree that heaven has issued to help us accelerate our ascension process. It is necessary for us to learn how to ask for their help and to use the power of our intent. The light beings that help us are always with us. We learn in these clearings how to use our intuition to ask questions and follow the prompting coming through our heart centers. We learn how to use MRT, pendulums, or our own inner knowing to confirm the insights of our intuition.

The holistic lifestyle is simply allowing ourselves to be connected to the Creator-Source. You allow yourself to recognize that when you get off track from the higher frequencies of love and light, you feel bogged down in the same old negative banter of your ego. You come to realize the energy of your beloved angels and guides will always come when you call them. By getting into your breathing, you can expand your energy and rise up into the higher frequencies; it is here you can feel their loving energies and receive messages from them.

Once you start communing with Creator-Source through your heart center connection, raising your level of consciousness and calling in your guidance teams, you won't find it acceptable to let yourself go back to the old patterns that you thought were safe. It will be easier for you to stay on course with where your process is taking you. It is always by observing your thoughts and feelings that you will see when you are going back into the lower vibrations.

When we clear the core fear matrix and negative programs, we realize that if we let them, the lower vibrations will trap us in the same loop of drama and fear, which is the nature of duality. When we allow ourselves to experience the higher dimensions, we come to know that the true nature of who we are is one of being in a state of love and joy, feeling our connection to Creator-Source, and accessing the unity consciousness of the One we all are.

In the realization of being the One we all are, we are connected with each other and our teams in the higher levels of consciousness; there is no separation. The ego isn't used at this point—it is in the background. We've never really been apart from each other and Creator-Source. It is just the illusion that the act of being inside of a human body is real. We are the actors and actresses, but it is all just an illusion.

People are going to have the session that the higher aspects of their being guide them to partake in, when they do the spirited clearings. They will each get something different out of their session.

If you have a session, and the negative program that deals with power and control is cleared, you are going to give yourself the opportunity for a fresh start in your relationships. You won't feel like running out the same thoughts and feelings that you used to control others or further enable others to control you; the fear around this issue will be cleared. It is up to you to let the energetic structure of this new dynamic take hold. The same words that used to trigger negative emotions won't magnetize you as easily as they did in the past. It will be up to you to let go, rise up into the higher frequencies, and create something that will serve you in your best and highest interests.

Doing the clearings will free up energy for you, because the amount of energy people use to keep the negative programming in place is huge—it is like living in a box acting out the same patterns and probabilities over and over again. When you let go of the old programs, then new energy comes in; you have the potential to bring in more of the light and love you really are. You are not only removing the immediate problem, but you are also providing yourself with the momentum to create whatever it is that you desire. You are removing the barriers and turning the tide, so that what stirs deep within you can rise to the top and carry you forward on your path.

It doesn't matter how long you have been struggling with problems in your life, or how serious they may seem to you; by uniting the bodies of your being with your guidance teams in this universal way, you are enabling yourself to accelerate and forge ahead in your ascension.

The spirited clearings help you harness the tools of your uplifting. These clearings are not just a one-off type of thing. You incorporate your gifts with the gifts you are being given by the light beings by committing yourself to a lifestyle of connection. This is an ongoing process. It is so true that whenever we rise up in vibration, we help the whole of creation to rise up into higher frequencies of light and love, and we raise the level of consciousness.

It is true that many of us who have come to this point of awakening (about who we are and what our purpose in life is) know that whatever issues we are endeavoring to clear, we are not just doing it for ourselves. When we free ourselves of negative programs, based in fear, we are helping others to turn on the light of their truth and rise up, to confront the obstacles that have been thwarting them; we are blazing the trail for them. As we have been inspired by others, such as the light beings who help us with these clearings, we shall also inspire others.

No matter how big the changes are that you are being called upon to make, taking out one program at a time, releasing the core fear matrix, and doing the present life cleanse will give you immediate results. When we do the clearings, we are communing with the light beings and the higher aspects of our own being; we are bringing higher frequencies of love and light into our being. These clearings will give you the momentum to unravel the layers of programming that the dark forces have orchestrated within the collective consciousness over many millennia.

The old saying is strike while the iron is hot. Now the light is finally dominant on our mother earth. Through lifetimes of service, we have helped this planet rise up in vibration. Changes are apparent in our reality that the old structures are crumbling from within. Instead of this being a time of fear, it is important for us to use what we have learned from many lifetimes of being the trailblazers on earth. We have chosen to follow the light of love and be in service to the One. We have acquired a stockpile of gifts and tools that are being called into play, so we can help ourselves and Mother Gaia ascend into the higher dimensions.

Dogmas

Mind-control programs can be subtle and not so subtle. The handlers attach themselves to us and set us up with thoughts that trigger our emotions, so that we become trapped in a loop of playing out the same behavior patterns. The ego, which feeds on fear, makes itself the main focus. These negative programs keep on feeding on us, and through us they are also set up to feed on others.

Doing the clearings enables us to jump out of the box of limitations that those programs saddle us with, and they enable us to access the truth of our hearts to create from a place of connection with who we really are. All it takes is putting out the intent to co-create these clearings with our teams.

Dogmas are beliefs we get imprinted with in religions, schools, financial institutions, the healthcare industry, the entertainment industry, the media, and more. They have been created in such a way as to program us with certain acceptable standards to which we must conform. The dogmas of these institutions are underpinned by fear and confusion, saying that this is the way things have to be, and they reinforce beliefs of right and wrong within us. The people who are the controllers of the money supply and the institutions realize that if the population doesn't adhere to their codes of control, then they will lose their power.

One dogma is that we are born in original sin. Another dogma is that we have to have our money printed on the printing presses of the Federal Reserve Board, which automatically puts us in debt. Another is that doctors know more about our bodies than we do. The theme of these dogmas is that there is a power greater than us who is against us, and we have to obey laws in order to appease that power.

Dogmas are beliefs that are designed to shift the balance of power to the controllers. Dogmas are encoded into the system for the shelter of elite families, providing the framework of lies that empower the institutions. The dogmas propagate fear, and they must not be challenged lest the wizard's curtain drop down to expose the whole charade. For instance, we may not think of the media as an institution that is controlled by the dark forces, but if we trace who funds them with advertising and who controls their licenses, then the picture becomes clear: they are interconnected to a vast structure that holds this negative programming in place. We have come to realize their agenda of fear and control has been in place for quite some time, and that it has been benefitting the same few elite families for many centuries.

If we think back to when we were young and in school, and how the beliefs of others influenced us, we realize that there was pressure to fit in and not rock the boat. A significant part of this programming manifests as dogmas. There also have been negative programs, devices, implants, vows, and disruptors designed by the dark ones to keep us in place, so that the dark ones could continue their reign of power over the earth.

The dogma-buster team of angels with their transmutable, blazing blue swords morph into vacuum cleaners to extract the dogmas from our crown chakras and transmute their energy to the higher vibrations of love and light. It is as simple as that. Our intent, along with the love we are and the help of the light beings, are a powerful tool to lift us up into higher realms of consciousness.

Curses

We can think of Guido of the light as this bright, shining being up in the higher dimensions who, along with his legions of angels, helps us to root out curses that keep us trapped in the lower vibrations. He removes both the curses that have been made on us and the ones we have made on others. He is a master builder who makes pathways that are sure to carry the light and find their way into your heart by removing the barriers and obstacles of this physical dimension, so that these higher light frequencies can penetrate your heart. You can think of Guido as the foreman, and his angels are his building crew. It's as if your heart is the temple and the shrine of your being. He makes sure that no impurities prevent the light and love from coming in and taking their place in the sanctuary of your heart.

Curses are a trick of the dark ones. Handlers use curses to attach themselves to us; the dark ones try to control us and trap our minds into having us play out a loop of fear. When others place curses on us, it gives them a false sense of power because they think they are in some way controlling or taking away power from beings whom they perceive as their enemies or not their equals.

This is not the way of the new energy of the higher dimensions. Curses are part of an agenda based in fear. Guido and his team of angels help us to keep our hearts pure and build founts of light to ensure our vessel of pure love stays in its integrity.

The PEMS Layers

All of us have four bodies to our being: the physical, emotional, mental, and spiritual (abbreviated together as PEMS). You can think of these bodies as layers or aspects of your being. It is with our connection in our heart centers that we learn how to balance these four bodies of our being.

All of us are interdimensional beings who exist in and out of linear time. There are different aspects of our being in this lifetime, such as our inner child, teenager, young adult, middle-aged self, elder, and more. There are also parallel dimensions of reality. Now the timelines of past, and future are merging into this Now moment, as we collectively bring in more light and the level of consciousness rises.

From the double helix model of DNA, we are evolving once more into a complex model of at least twelve strands. We are going from being carbon based to crystalline based. Our brains have been rewired to accommodate these higher frequencies, by activating parts of the brain that have been dormant for a very long time. These parts of the brain correspond to what scientists have called "junk DNA." Our DNA has within itself a map of who we are and who we've been. All of us have lived many lifetimes; we have been tested time and time again with different issues and life lessons. There is always an originating lifetime where a negative program started, where the handlers came in and manipulated us in some way to feed themselves with negative programming. Fear is always at the root of their programs to enslave us. Fear is a total disconnect from Creator-Source, and this leaves us open to being taken over by their negative programming.

Time as we know it in the third dimension is linear. The more we rise up in vibration, the more we come to know that the past, present, and future exist in the Now moment, and what we do affects all points on the timeline. When we do our housecleaning, it is for the totality of our being, across all timelines in all parallel dimensions and universes. None of the lower vibrations can come with us into the higher dimensions that we are rising up into as we ascend with Mother Gaia.

Each one of us has been conditioned by the beliefs we have carried around. Our beliefs have been formed by a web of negative programming that has kept us at low consciousness levels for many lifetimes. In doing the clearings and using MRT, we pinpoint the lifetime in which these programs originated, and this enables us to clear them all across the board of parallel lifetimes and dimensions throughout the PEMS layers of our being.

When we allow ourselves to go to the higher interdimensional levels of our being, we go into a place of trust and inner knowing, a place where all emotions are born out of love and light. We transcend the limits of the mind and allow ourselves to feel the purity of higher consciousness, which we in our divinity are. The more that our journey through this life reflects on and focuses on the love we are, the more we are able to take in the higher light codes, which make it harder for those of the darkness to control not just us but the whole of creation.

You can think of the process of doing the clearings as a way of making more space for the higher frequencies of love and light to come in. We do this by clearing what has been keeping us in the same patterns of fear. The clearings facilitate an unimpeded flow of universal love with the higher aspects of our being. The connection we have with Creator-Source is realized and maintained through our conscious intent for the bodies of our being to be centered in our heart, balanced with the transmission and reception of higher light codes through the pineal gland.

The spirited clearings are a co-creation with the unseen light beings. When we merge with them to remove the negative programs based in fear, we rise up into their level of high vibration and become entrained with them. Truly on the interdimensional levels of our being, we are One.

There are only two emotions, fear and love. Fear has many names to it, such as anger, envy, jealousy, and revenge. Love is grounded in all of the higher vibrations such as appreciation, forgiveness, joy, allowance, acceptance, understanding, compassion, and gratitude. When you accept that your thoughts and emotions create your reality and that you are responsible for them, you will come to understand that you are a creator. The more responsibility that you allow yourself to take for your creations, the freer you become and the more you are able to reflect the truth of your connection to your divinity and Oneness to Creator-Source.

The law of attraction is a universal law that states anything you focus on expands. If you raise your vibration up into the high frequencies of love and light, magic is very possible. The universe wants to help you to get what you ask for. The more you focus on what you want to create in love, forgiveness, compassion, and gratitude as if it has already happened, the easier it is to bring it into your reality.

Each of us is infinite energy, and we are eternal; there is no time. Linear time is a construct of this 3-D hologram that we have created in the schoolhouse of planet earth. It is up to each of us to own our creations; all of us created this physical 3-D reality to experience duality. When we own and accept that the hologram of this creation is an illusion, it truly is a liberating experience. Knowing this gives us the perspective that we are all equally derived from the One, the source of creation, and that there has never been any separation from Creator-Source. This is so because when we are without bodies, we are united with the higher aspects of our being. In this place of unity and consciousness with our "I Am" presence, we are all integral parts of the godhead.

Beliefs have been planted within our being. They were part of mass consciousness, and we, because we are part of the collective consciousness, were responsible for constructing them in the way we did. They served a purpose in the lower vibrations when survival was the key; these belief systems were responsible for getting us to the place we are now. We have come to realize that the reality we created from using them no longer serves us.

Now we are fully in step with the dance of ascension, bringing in the new energy. The new energy is a reflection of our higher consciousness, which is coinciding with us transforming from carbon-based to crystalline-based consciousness. We are now more connected with Creator-Source than we ever have been before. The light has become dominant, and many people are waking up from the illusion.

It is up to each one of us to not allow ourselves to be controlled by the media and entertainment industries. It is up to us to pull in the frequencies of love and light, which give us messages of how to accelerate the ascension of this planet and all of the beings on it. We also may ask for signs from our teams to show us if we are going in the direction we intend.

Listening and trusting in the messages and signs we get bring us to the heart of who we are. When we allow ourselves to be in our heart centers, pure of heart, and when we open up our third eye, which is also known as the pineal gland, we strengthen the connection to Creator-Source, shining and radiating this connection out to the All That Is.

When we give intent to access our own inner truth, we connect with a higher interdimensional part of our being. All of us play an integral part in the unity of the One, and each of us has our own role to play in this divine undertaking, as do the unseen light beings and the interdimensional aspects of our being.

Our barometer for knowing if we are in alignment with our truth is the way it feels. Using the tool of MRT is paramount in affirming data. When we are connected in our hearts, we receive and transmit the higher frequencies of Creator-Source.

Imagination

When we develop and use our imagination, it helps us to live outside the box that we were conditioned to believe we needed to inhabit in order to survive within the confines of duality. It is up to us to use the wings of our heart to carry us high within our creations, to cast off the limits of the ego mind, and to give free reign to our inner knowing.

When we go to this deep and free place, we access the part of our DNA that allows us to bring in the archives of the collective consciousness. In this place of deep inspiration, we work at the subatomic level. We have access to many transmissions from Creator-Source. In this place of unity we are free to call upon the memories and perceptions of who we are and where we've been; the multi-verses are available to us to create our masterpieces in.

As there is no space and time, we are able to see that all experiences, thoughts, and perceptions exist in the Now. This is the place where we experience ourselves and the multi-verses as one with the All That Is.

I ask you to consider that all things are possible and that in each moment we have the possibility to be born anew. It is as simple as seeing things from a different perspective, or what the Toltec shamans call the assemblage point. When you shift the assemblage point, you find new possibilities, new information, and new ways of processing it. These transmissions of information from the Source come in through our heart centers.

When we expand our consciousness by expanding the energy in our heart center and our pineal gland, we allow ourselves to receive vast amounts of universal love, and the connection with Creator-Source through our teams becomes clearer. The quality of the information increases because the frequencies of light and love rise up.

It is in the right lobe of the brain where connections are made that enable us to access higher dimensions of reality. Our intuition lets us filter what we are receiving from our guidance teams; we use our gift of discernment to know what information is nurturing us. It always comes back to our emotional guidance system, which means that the higher vibrations and frequencies of love and light are always going to feel good, and of course these higher frequencies allow us to create our reality in a way that is in alignment with our divine nature. MRT, pendulums, and our inner knowing play a key role in allowing ourselves to discern the info we are getting.

We can always bring in the teams we work with, such as the violet flame angels and Archangel Amethyst, to encase us in their brilliant light for protection from handlers. Our imagination is the vehicle we use to let the free spirit of our soul soar in the revelations we are asking for.

Some of us will be able to see, hear, or feel things from the higher dimensions; many artists are able to do this and create wonderful manifestations of the love we all are. We all channel to some degree, but it is up to us how much we allow ourselves to bring in these higher frequencies of love and light to create bridges and pathways for ourselves and others.

In our meditations the gift and art of imagination helps us to feel the glory of the love we all are. Allowing ourselves to be sensitive to vibrations of higher light will help us to receive transmissions from our guidance teams, who want to be rejoined with us. They can't cross the line and go against our free will and make the reality for us, but we can call them in as co-creators by using our power of intent. When we use and develop our imagination, we interpret the magnificence of their realms of light and allow them to shine within our minds and hearts.

Being open, and not judging ourselves or expecting the experience of communing in the higher vibrations to be any particular thing or to feel any certain way, is pivotal for us in taking responsibility for our creations. Gratitude and having a sense of wonder and delight helps us stay connected to Creator-Source. This connection is the conduit of our inspiration from which we receive messages and transmissions of unconditional love and unbridled joy.

Using our imagination—along with our intuition, when we are doing spirited clearing sessions with ourselves or our clients—will help us and our clients to feel the connection with who we really are: the divine, higher aspects of our being.

Whatever we experience with our interdimensional senses, when we call in our teams of guides and angels, we can be assured that that on some level or dimension of reality, what we are experiencing is real.

In this time of ascension it is upon us to answer the call and keep ourselves raised up in the light. We are not alone in our journey and have many unseen beings of light to help us in this glorious ascent from the third dimension into the fifth dimension and beyond.

We are the bridge builders, the trail blazers, and when we accept our roles within this game of life we are playing at this time of great shift and upliftment, we have a magnanimous effect on the whole of creation.

Chapter 2

Victim or Victor?

The Game of Duality

In a session of spirited clearings, you want to look at what you are feeling inside, or if you are doing a session or conference call, you want the client or participants to acknowledge what they feel. You want to open up to what is going on inside; this means seeing what triggers fear within yourself or the people with which you are working. Many times this means experiencing feelings that don't feel good. There may be times in your life that seemed very "down in the dumpies," as Ashtar says. It is important to look at these feelings and what was going on at those times.

It is only by allowing yourself to feel these lower vibrations and to look at what caused them that you can see what you were permitting to come into your life. All of us design the blueprints of our lives to include certain experiences. All of us wanted to be here, especially at this time of ascension, to have these certain experiences that help our souls evolve.

All of us have been playing out this interdimensional, cosmic game of being a human for many thousands of years. We knew that this lifetime held great promise for us (humans and Mother Gaia and her kingdoms) to ascend as a whole. This lifetime was seen as our collective chance to bring the game of duality to completion in a very beautiful, harmonious way.

Like any of the lifetimes we had on earth, where we were playing out duality, all of us agreed we were going to come down here and deal with the illusion of the hologram and the veil that was locked into place to shut out memories and any conscious connection with other aspects of our being in the higher dimensions. We gave ourselves experiences in the densest part of the duality to heal, and it was up to us to stay out of separation from Creator-Source, so that by shining our light and love, we could one day remember who we were and collectively rise up into the fifth dimension, where none of the lower vibrations that we were playing out in duality would be present.

It doesn't matter how you believe that any of these scenarios of bringing this game of duality to completion were designed in the higher dimensions, how they have affected us, or will be affecting us. What does matter is that in this Now moment we all have the opportunity to take responsibility for creating ourselves in a human body and the world around us, and to raise the level of our vibration and, in doing so, liberate ourselves into the golden age of the fifth dimension on Mother Gaia.

Anytime we feel the love and light we are and spread it out to the universe, we raise the level of consciousness of the All That Is. We are connected in our heart centers to, and are one with, the All That Is, to Creator-Source. In this moment of knowing, we are love and light, we are the victors over fear.

I feel that shining our light and being the love we are is the main reason why we are here. By being who we are and not going for the illusion of separation, we help others to remember and be who they are. When we are beaming love and light, we help others not get caught in their ego, and we remind them not to go for fear. The efforts of the dark forces who have plied us with devices and programs of mind control, to keep us in the lower vibrations and basically to be slaves to their masters as well as themselves, are all rendered ineffective when we shine our lights of love on them and their endeavors.

Fear is their master tool. Fear is the weapon they wield that is capable of severing our connection to the Creator-Source. The way we take back the reigns of creating our experience of being who we really are is to look at what we have created in our lives. It is necessary to be able to own our creations and discern for ourselves what purpose we intended when we created them. When we created these experiences, what gift did we intend to give ourselves?

Sometimes we create things with our soul to bring out intense feelings within us. We tend to push ourselves to see what we can achieve under pressure. We may design our experiences in a way that we will be given chance after chance to change our choices and responses to the obstacles we have created for ourselves. We may have grappled with some of these choices lifetime after lifetime.

It is only when we reach a place of acceptance of why we have created the same results from happening in our life over and over again that we can let go of them by choosing to clear them. When we clear the negative energy that was causing us to attach to the choices and outcomes, we transmute the lower vibrations into higher frequencies of love and light. When we come to realize we can make different choices that will not repeat the same behavior patterns, we can manifest a different, higher vibrating, and more fulfilling reality for ourselves. We can be most happy and grateful when we clear negative programs and bless our experience and ourselves for healing a layer of the programming that has been holding us back.

It Is Never the Other Person

Many of us are programmed to blame others for the results we experience. We are programmed to think blaming others lets us off of the hook for the thoughts we think, the words we say, and the actions we do—which not only create our reality, but also influence the collective consciousness and the larger sphere of reality it creates. Many of us project the judgments we have on our reality onto others. We say it is this or that person who is always giving us a hard time. We say the other person is the reason why we can't concentrate; the other person always makes a mess, and we have to clean it up; the other person makes our life at work miserable; the other person cheats and gets away with it, and it isn't fair. When we project our negative emotions onto others, we mire ourselves in negativity, and it multiplies on us. Nothing stays stagnant in the universe; whatever we focus on expands.

When we focus on what someone else does and project our negative emotions onto it, power is taken away from us. We don't have to know or be concerned with anyone else's life experience; their movie is not our movie, so we don't have to be concerned or feel responsible for it. By focusing on their negativity, we are just focusing on negativity in general, and this gives us and the All That Is nothing more than more negativity. It's up to us to raise the level of our vibration by bringing in the highest frequencies of love and light by focusing on the love we are and the wonder of creation and the splendor of being here at this time of us ascending into the fifth dimension.

None of us have to react to anything in a certain way. No one is making us angry; we are choosing to react that way. We don't have to feed the polarity by allowing ourselves to be triggered by what someone else is doing. We are not the target of their negative vibrations; it is up to us to know we are always one with the All That Is. Everything else our mind tells us is a lie, and it is up to us to drive our vehicle and not have it drive us.

We are the ones who set the frequency level of our vibration. We are a free-will planet, and it is up to us to tune into the highest frequency that aligns with and is connected to Creator-Source. It is up to us to be in our heart centers. We always have the choice to go for the disconnection of being in fear or pulling in the high vibes of love and light.

Denial

The program of denial figures into this equation when we try to convince ourselves we don't need to change anything, and yet we tell ourselves we deserve different results. If we are in denial about the effects of what we are creating, there is no reason to change our choices or our feelings about our issues. We may still be blaming someone or something else, or thinking that it just doesn't matter.

It is only by raising the level of our vibration and connecting in our heart centers that we will be guided to make choices that will enable us to let go of the negativity and fear that our egos feed on and bring these issues to completion, by healing them with unconditional, universal love.

We can think of the ego as narcissistic. The ego in effect is saying, "Yes, I am special, and this can't happen to me. I can do the same things others do, and yet I will be spared of the results they receive when they do these things, because I am smarter, I am more beautiful, God/Goddess loves me more than the others, I have better connections, and I have more money." The ego can be thought of as the snake that tempted Eve in the Bible story of the fall from grace in the Garden of Eden. If you let it, the ego will flatter and subvert you with its drama, but when the cycle of drama plays out, you will find that it has been feeding off your fear.

There is a place inside the bodies of our being that I tend to think of as the point of truth. We have to be inside of our bodies by being connected to Creator-Source through our heart centers. It is here at this point of truth that we connect with our "I Am" presence and allow ourselves to be sovereign. It is our place of balance, and we connect with our inner knowing here.

No matter how we try to circumvent this place of knowing, our experiences in life will still keep bringing us back to it. I feel that we are guided here by our angels and ascended masters. It is up to us to really want to know our truth, and when we fully accept the sound and feeling of truth within our being, we will make choices that will enable us to raise the level of our vibration, and we will attract what we truly desire in our lives.

It is up to us to liberate ourselves from the fear, which is the basis of the survival programming we have been imprinted with since birth. We do this by following the guidance of our spiritual team; this takes being courageous and being connected in our heart center to trust our intuition and guides, which sometimes manifest as the small voice whispering to us inside our heads. It takes imagination and heart to know just how marvelous we truly are. We must love and respect ourselves greatly to bust out of the box of the programs we have been imprinted with. Until we do this, we stay the victim to the dark forces who have created these programs.

We Are Indissoluble

When we say we didn't create our reality—that is, we are saying we didn't create the car crash we were in, we didn't create that low grade we got on the last test, we weren't responsible for making that man punch us and break our nose, we didn't create the cancer spreading throughout our body—we are saying there was someone or something else that was responsible for making it happen. This is the logic of being the victim. When we know we have co-created everything that happens to us in our reality, we know we are an integral, indissoluble part of the All That Is. It is up to us to know we gave permission to be here, and when we did so, we gave permission for everything that happens to us in this lifetime. This makes us co-creators of our reality.

We all came into this level of duality on a free-will planet, knowing it would be quite a challenge to find our way home. We knew the level of density was so thick that we would be cut off from knowing the story of why we came here, how we came to be in this physical body, who we were before we came here, how what we do affects the whole of creation, and what roles we played in past lives, and what roles people in this life played with us in past lives.

All of these things seem to be mysteries to us, but when we allow ourselves to know that we are interdimensional beings who have a soul, we know we are always connected to the creator. We know each and every one of us is an indissoluble part of the All That Is. We know we are all One.

By being connected in our heart centers, we allow ourselves to feel and be our inner essence. We enable ourselves to commune with this place of inner knowing and Oneness. Our heart center is a place of connection to Creator-Source, and it is a place of unconditional, universal love. It is where we access the true essence of our being, which is the highest level of vibration to which we can rise. All of creation is born from this unconditional, universal love; we are all united as One in the higher dimensions of our being.

Now as I write this, we are at a place of evolution within our species and on our planet where we are ascending to full consciousness inside our bodies. It is up to us to remove the negative programming, which in its broadest sense includes curses, vows, dogmas, devices, implants, entities, disrupter energy, negative programs and replicators, dendrites, and more. These are some of the main ways the dark forces have kept us in fear. When we are in fear, we cannot tap into the place of connection and Oneness. We can't raise our level of vibration when we are afraid. It takes our conscious choice to raise the level of our vibration, and by doing this it is possible for us to take back the power of our being sovereign, from which their negative programs have cut us off.

The Lists

When we wrestle with why our reality doesn't feel good. When we think about why we feel abandoned and shut off from the ones we love, why some people seem to be so gifted and have so much more than us, and why some things never seem to affect others in the painful way they affect us, then we are allowing our egos to feed on us. We are going for our ego's rationalized insanity, which feeds on separation and multiplies layer upon layer of negative programming.

The law of attraction ensures the level of the vibration we are emitting will attract a matching vibration into our reality. If you ask for abundance but have thoughts that doubt how you could create a reality that is abundant, then you won't bring the level of abundance into your reality that you are asking for, because the level of your vibration doesn't match it.

It is like you are driving a car to the store to receive your abundance, but on the way there you keep stepping on the brakes, so you never quite get there. It is like swimming upstream or taking one step forward and two steps backward. You will never get where you intend to go if you aren't completely in the higher vibrations of love, joy, and compassion.

It is up to us to tune into the highest vibrations of love and light. It is up to us to know we are worthy of receiving all that we ask. It is up to us not to judge ourselves or others, but to forgive ourselves and the others who have co-created fear and patterns of this negative programming with us.

We are all set up with negative programming. Giving into the fear that is the underlying foundation of all of those negative belief systems enables the same behavior patterns to manifest the same results. These are results we are not consciously intending, but because we are not consciously creating in the higher frequencies of love and light, and because we focus on our limitations, we will receive something that matches the level of our vibration, which will be less than what we are asking to come into our physical reality.

All of us would like to change what doesn't feel good in our lives. Many of us don't really believe it is possible; it feels as if there is something that is always popping up that is holding us back, some sort of unseen obstacle. We can think of this as what we are holding onto in our subconscious. This negativity that we are holding onto is an unseen influence that causes us to vibrate at a level that is not in alignment with our desires, and it causes us to make choices that don't vibrate in the highest levels of love and light.

These unseen influences are the negative programming, entities, devices, and implants; that in many cases we have been carrying around from lifetime to lifetime. Just think of how many lifetimes we all have had of running around and banging our heads against the wall of illusion, by struggling with these same issues. It is common knowledge that most of the issues we are dealing with have been with us before in past lives.

The paradox is that we don't even have to think of these things as ours. When we come right down to what we are dealing with, all of us have given permission to be here at this time to clear these negative behavior patterns that keep on creating the same results in which separation is manifested. When we clear this negativity, we raise the level of light for All That Is. Duality is drawing to a close, because the light is now so dominant on the planet that it allows us to bring in the higher frequencies that will return us to the fifth dimension and speed us along in our ascension process.

Now we are at the place of evolution in our lives and of the planet where we can let go of the karma once and for all that we as a collective consciousness have created in duality. We have played out the creation of duality to its most dense manifestations; our graduation time is here.

It is up to us to raise the level of vibration to this next higher dimension, where none of the lower vibrations can exist. This will allow us to create through unity consciousness. This is a place where the ego is not a controlling factor anymore.

In the higher light frequencies of the fifth dimension, our needs will be taken care of, so the ego won't be necessary as a function of our survival. The whole model of duality that we have collectively given permission to exist will now transmute into one where the power of our intent will not have barriers to manifesting our desires.

Many of us moan in agony, thinking that we can never change the things we feel are too overwhelming in our lives. Some of us are fighting diseases that sap the strength out of us, such as cancer, multiple sclerosis, dementia, cystic fibrosis, fibromyalgia, and more. Some of us think we will never get out of debt or get a job that pays well and that we love to do.

Knowing that you gave permission for all of these things to surface in your life is the first step to empowering yourself. When you empower yourself by owning your creations, in that moment you are the victor, and nothing can take away your power. You know that there is nothing to be afraid of, because you know that any feelings or perceptions of being separate from Creator-Source are an illusion. You gave permission to be part of this holographic illusion, where your love would be tested time and time again. You gave permission for these challenges to be in your life, and you own that you can uncreate them, whatever they are.

In dealing with all of these lists that the mind can get stuck thinking about in a negative way, I would love you to bring in the attitude of gratitude and allow yourself to feel again anytime in this life where you have felt joy, love, satisfaction, relief, and success. Feel grateful for all these times and all you have taken part in by being here in a human body at this time of ascension.

We uncreate the obstacles and challenges in our lives by recognizing when negative thoughts come in and what feeling we associate to them. We train ourselves not to focus on these thoughts, but to acknowledge them in love and light and be the observer or witness of them. If we allow ourselves to see the unfolding process of these negative thoughts, we know the result will bring more negativity into our being and create situations that don't serve us.

We can think of it as switching channels or just saying no as soon as we recognize where the thought and feeling that it comes with is going to take us. We can replace the negative thought with one that is born of gratitude and love, or we can just be neutral. We want to condition ourselves to focus on what feels good and nurtures us; by doing this we will thrive and reconnect with our true divine nature.

Resistance

The pain that arises in our lives, whether it is physical, emotional, mental, or spiritual, is because we have resistance. Yes, it us up to us to allow ourselves to know what we are resisting. Anytime we feel that we aren't at peace, that we are in pain of any kind, that we are not in a place of love or acceptance, we are resisting. This creates tension, which builds into pain because it has no outlet. It eats away at whatever area of the bodies of our being we are storing this tension.

Many of us have resistance to working at a job that is not our passion. Instead of giving into anger and frustration and thoughts that feed the resistance, we can accept and be grateful for how the job is serving us in our lives, and how it is a stepping stone to having a livelihood where we are doing something about which we are passionate. This process of accepting what we are doing for work means that we allow ourselves to be in the Now moment and not get caught up in thinking about the past and future. This Now moment is timeless, eternal, and if we allow ourselves to go deeply into it, we will remind ourselves of our divine nature.

If we don't allow ourselves to be our divine nature, and we allow ourselves to be caught up in our thoughts trying to figure things out, it can feel as if we are trapped and that it will never end. We convince ourselves we are trapped by settling for a job that will pay the bills but not give us the type of fulfillment we are seeking. When we focus on what we don't have, we will continue to get what we don't have. When we feel as if what we have asked for has already come into our lives, we feel peace and balance, enabling what we are asking for to manifest into our reality.

Many of us are in depressed states because the repetitiveness of our existence overwhelms us. Tasks such as doing the dishes, paying the bills, buying groceries, taking out the garbage, and cleaning our living spaces can seem totally unnecessary to us. We face tasks and challenges day after day just to be able to feel safety and peace, just to be able to get through today to get to tomorrow. Where our prospects seem to be none the better, it can cause us to ponder the fruitlessness of our situation. When we allow ourselves to be in the lower vibrations, negative programs can get triggered.

Many people turn to drugs to ward off depression. There is nothing outside of ourselves that can assuage and soothe us—the answer comes from within. When we allow ourselves to come to a place of knowing, there is a much bigger picture to our existence at this time, and every time we feel love, every time we laugh, every time we allow ourselves to be in nature and feel the oneness of creation, we are moving energy, we are raising the level of the vibration, we are shining the light, and we are blazing the trail for others on their path of ascension. We are the victors whenever we expand our love and light outward to the rest of creation.

When we want to create our desires, it is as simple as changing our thoughts and emotions and making different choices. All of us must recognize that we have been programmed to be afraid of doing things that we haven't done before. We have the opportunity to create a new dialogue to prepare ourselves for taking the first step in any enterprise. Instead of feeling doubt, we can allow ourselves to think of this new experience as an opportunity to learn. It is up to us to exercise the tool of patience and adapt ourselves to this new situation by finding the rhythm, timing, and synchronization to put the steps together and form a process that will let us find the desired end result.

When we see that we have created a certain way of dealing with bringing a task to successful completion, we can allow ourselves to savor this moment in our cycle of creation. We can see that even though the task may have taken some repetition and effort on our part, we have come up with a way to apply ourselves by paying attention to the details. We didn't let the process shift our focus into a lower vibrating space of anger when we felt overwhelmed. Even if we did, we forgave ourselves for our resistance and we got back to the task, maybe with a new perspective of why we felt discomfort over doing it. We had a feeling of gratitude for what we were experiencing and learning about ourselves by going through all of the steps that the process of bringing the task to completion brought us.

We can feel satisfaction that we tried our best and allowed ourselves to be in the Now without attaching to the outcome. We can feel a fullness and wholeness of the All That Is in giving into its rhythm, timing, and synchronization. We allowed ourselves to flow with the demands of this new situation, and we celebrate every facet of the experience, which now is not new anymore. It is no longer stressful thinking about and doing the task, because now we have a handle on it; we blazed the trail for ourselves. Now we are able to focus on the different parts of the process, knowing them and understanding them, so the total endeavor no longer seems beyond our grasp.

We tell ourselves that once we get over the fear of doing this new thing or beginning a relationship with this new person, then we will have a foundation to grow upon. Even if we don't get it the first time, it is just a matter of time before we learn from our mistakes. Then we will get it, and we will have learned how to do one more thing—and this wouldn't have come about if we hadn't made the choice of trying and applying ourselves.

All we have to do is to be willing to try, to allow ourselves to be open and not judge ourselves for trying to do something new. When we feel ourselves going into judgment, we know that fear is trying to dominate our focus. It is necessary for us to accept ourselves as divine parts of the whole of creation and to know that all of creation emanates out of and is derived from universal, unconditional love.

When we breathe consciously and feel the connection in our hearts to Creator-Source, accepting what we are creating consciously allowing, ourselves to be in the flow of divine energy and balanced within the four bodies of our being, it feels good to be connected to the All That Is. There is no worry, doubt, or judgment that will pop up when we are at this place of connection in our heart centers. This is where and when we are not resisting.

When we are listening to uplifting music, drawing or painting a picture, or doing anything that we love to do, we are not resisting being in this Now moment. We are allowing ourselves to be in the eternal flow of love and light we are.

The veil is still in place on earth, but by our efforts to raise the level of vibration of energy, we will eventually lift the veil. The light is becoming more dominant every day. Portals and crystals and zero-point energy tools that have not been activated for thousands of years are once again coming online and being utilized. It is with the power of intent that we infuse our love and light into these energy centers and tools, either alone or with the focused intent of others. When we do this, we accelerate the ascension process.

Until the veil comes down, we won't fully know what part we are playing in the grand scheme of this story of creation, which we have been co-creating for many thousands of years. We won't see how we or the people we love have affected the whole of creation. We won't see how we influence people through our strength, courage, and kindness. We won't know the full story of the difference we make. We have been working many lifetimes toward bringing Mother Gaia and ourselves into the fifth dimension where none of the lower vibrations will exist any longer.

It is up to us to be in love and gratitude for the role we are playing in helping ourselves and the planet ascend. It is just a simple change in the way we perceive the human condition that can cause us to take responsibility for being here and inspire us to liberate ourselves from being the victim of the negative programming that has enabled the dark forces to have power over us and the Earth for such a long time.

The Gift of Giving

Who hasn't dreamed of being able to give those we love something we know they wanted? Do we let ourselves be stopped from giving, if we don't have all that the person is asking for? Giving is from the heart, and we can give with a smile or laughter, telling a story or listening to their dreams and aspirations, simply by allowing ourselves to be with the other person in love and acceptance.

I have asked myself what has held me back from giving freely. I hear all of my excuses as the observer, not allowing myself to give because of self-judgment. I know some of it had to do with being programmed with lack. I feel it is related to not trusting that Creator-Source provides for us, so we are hesitant to give what we have, thinking that we may be asked for more, or that we will one day run out of whatever we are giving. We worry we will be judged for giving of our being, for allowing ourselves to care, for seeing and treating others as our equals.

We can't really learn from being in the human condition unless we allow ourselves to be in the present moment so totally and unconditionally that we let go to our heart's desires. I am not saying that we need to be frivolous, but we can let ourselves drink fully in the love of our heart and go for the feeling that is propelling the impulse to give of ourselves and of what we have to others. We must consider the degree of liberation we can feel when we no longer listen to the fear programming and let go of our attachments to limiting beliefs, so we can freely give of our money, time, talents, and various expressions of love to others. We can acknowledge the great sense of gratitude we have in being in a position to contribute our gifts to others. Perhaps you feel that you are One with everything that is. Perhaps you live in your heart at least some of the time. You have been able to neutralize your programming to a certain degree; you are learning the ways of love when you identify and merge into the feeling of being connected to the All That Is. This is the place where no doubt or worry can creep in, where you can give without being attached to the outcome.

Clearing out the negative, transmuting the lower vibrations into the higher frequencies of love and light, and ushering in the positive is a lifestyle. It is allowing the feeling of love to permeate our being and allowing ourselves to know we are all beings derived from that love. Each of us is a unique ray or frequency of that love, and we cannot be duplicated.

Living inside of our bodies means balancing our hearts with our minds. We must aspire to having our minds be our servants instead of being slaves to our ego minds, which feed on fear and drama. Being connected in our heart centers is the main way to free ourselves and to fully initiate ourselves into the new energy. When we do, we allow ourselves to know we are sovereign beings of love and light. When we give, it must be from our hearts and firmly centered in the knowing we are One with all of creation; there is no separation. The Law of One states that if one is harmed, all are harmed, and when one is helped, all are helped.

If we can find the courage and strength to live in the Now and use the opportunities we are given to share our love and light, our efforts will exponentially affect the whole in a most positive way.

So much of our programming has to do with lack & self-protection; we think there is always someone or something that is looking for ways to harm us. We are taught that we must survive at all costs and that there is always someone or something that wants to take away what we need to survive.

When we start to let go of the weave of fear programming and unravel its matrix, we start to see how our emotions have been intertwined with negative thoughts, creating barriers for us. We all have been made to feel that we need to hide away and not invite anyone too closely into our lives, except maybe that special someone. We were taught that our privacy was sacred and should never be violated.

The impulses we were imprinted with directed us to live that way. This imprint process was a deep intertwining of thoughts and emotions that were fear based. The powers that have controlled the earth's resources, including our money supply for so long, use fear as their main weapon to keep us separated. When we come together in love, we possess the spiritual, higher dimensional power to create a reality that is in harmony with Mother Gaia. Nothing will be lacking or denied us in the higher frequencies to which we are ascending. First we must clean ourselves of the negative programming that has blocked our evolution; then we will be able to assimilate the higher frequencies, which will enable the changes necessary for the planet to ascend with us on it.

We must have peace on earth for us to ascend. When we choose to give from our hearts, whether it be money or any of the gifts we possess, we bust down the walls that prevent us from coming together and raising the level of consciousness. The old, bitter hatreds and feuds of one clan or one nation against another must be healed in the love we all are in order for the plan of our ascension to unfold.

In many instances the gift we will give to all of humanity will be forgiving ourselves for going for the pain of feeling separation in playing the game of life in this 3-D holographic illusion here on Mother Gaia. Letting go of the past and not allowing ourselves to be attached to the pain and heartbreak takes an opening, a blossoming of our heart centers. When this happens, it makes it easier for others to raise the level of their vibration also. We can only do this by forgiving ourselves and making the conscious choice to remove the negative programming that is holding us back. When we make a choice in alignment with positive change, it is a choice for the world to rise up in the highest frequencies of love and light, for us to come together as One. It is being done, but it requires all of us who have decided to ascend to bring the issues we are working on in this lifetime to completion. When we do this, we give up our pain, and we let go to our ascension process.

When we are faced with challenges, instead of going for the programmed response to be angry and blame someone or something for the pain we are feeling, we can remember we are all One, because the essence of our being is the love that unites us as integral, indissoluble parts of Creator-Source. We have the ability to forgive and love all of the challenges and obstacles to our freedom. We give ourselves the gift of compassion when we allow others to make their choices, and we don't judge them for it, even though their choices may adversely affect us.

We can be our truth. We can say what we feel without attachment to us being right and others being wrong. When we speak from our heart and see that this game of life is a play of illusion, and that it needs all of its characters to function in the purpose it was created for, we are in forgiveness for any perceived pain. Feeling separate from the Creator-Source causes us great pain; we shut ourselves off from the love of the Creator. When we see that we have given ourselves the opportunity to think, speak, and act in the knowing that we are always connected to Creator-Source, we are taking responsibility for being here and being the great creators we are.

Others may judge us for being freer in our actions than they are. We can bless them and send them light and love, because they are coming from the lower vibrations of fear. It takes courage for us to give of ourselves from our hearts—to give of our laughter, our stories, our songs, our dances, our insights.

This giving of love from our hearts opens the doors for us to access the abundance and wonder of who we really are. When we come together in love with one another in meditation, or by sending love to an area going through earth changes, there is an exponential quantum effect. In *Power vs. Force*, David Hawkins has stated that a conscious being sending forth its love and light can equal a thousand beings who are unconscious and not of the light. Whenever we come together to focus our love, the energy goes viral and raises the level of consciousness.

It all begins with just one of us. Now is the time of momentous change on our planet. The shift from being controlled by fear-based, negative programming in a survival-oriented reality to one where our passion and the truth of who we are as divine human angels of love and light is supported and nurtured, and where our abundance and our potential are unlimited comes into view—this is what the end of the Mayan Calendar in 2012 portends for us.

When we learn how to give unconditionally, we learn how to receive the support of the universe, and we learn how to receive from one another with an open heart. The law of attraction has been our ally, if we have allowed ourselves to feel the joy and blessings of our true nature. If we have not and have been mired in focusing on what we didn't have, it has been a great teacher nonetheless.

When we give, we let go to one another, and we let the possibilities of our time together shine forth in a rainbow of radiant sound and soothing, delightful colors. It is up to us to remember that each of us is an integral part of the godhead.

Taking Back the Power

"I recognize myself as a co-creator, and I now stand ready to clear whatever I have created as blocking my way." When we say this to the universe, we are preparing ourselves to get rid of the entities, programs, devices, and implants that are blocking us from ascending.

Each of us has some kind of routine we follow that keeps us in a place of feeling secure. It is up to us to realize how much we are limiting our creative potential by holding onto belief systems that form the same behavior patterns, which no longer serve us. For some it is using recreational drugs, drinking alcohol, eating sugar—and fat-laden foods, looking at pornography, watching movies or TV programs that keep us mired in the lower vibrations, and being obsessive about our use of new technology like computers and cell phones.

Any and all attachments keep us at a fixed vibrational level. The negative programs we have been imprinted with are designed to keep us in these lower vibrations. The ego feeds on our fears. Yes, many people will say they aren't afraid, but all of the lower vibrations are based in fear. There are only two emotions in the universe, love and fear. Being in a place of universal, unconditional love will let us appreciate what we have created, and from this space of awareness we see there is no reason to attach to or possess anything or anyone. It is all One, and each and every one of us are an integral part of creation.

Love is an expansive state of allowing ourselves to be in the "Now" moment. We allow ourselves to feel joy and to remember that our existence is all an illusion. We are grateful for the experiences we have within the context of this hologram. When we are in the state of universal, unconditional love, then we are flexible, nonjudgmental, accepting, allowing, forgiving, in gratitude, receptive, and neutral.

There are a lot of negative programs such as following orders, pleasing others, not getting enough sleep, and giving away our power to feel secure, to name a few. All of these programs were designed to keep us in place in the third dimension, which means that we were being held as a captive of duality.

Since I've been doing the spirited clearings that Meg originated, I've come to realize that we can be on either side of these negative programs. We can be the ones who were victimized, or we can be the ones who did the victimizing. Either way the same negative program has power over us, because the lower vibrations of the program have control over us by limiting our access to the higher frequencies. Even when we were victimizing people, fear was running rampant within our being.

Many of us were taken over by entities when we were doing drugs, or were involved in pornography, or were on the field of battle. Whenever we were in low vibrational places, there were handlers that came in to administer programs, implants, devices, or entities. The handlers placed these things in our subconscious, so it is very possible we didn't know we were carrying them around. Some of us carried around these types of negative programming for many lifetimes and in parallel realities.

The only way we become the victors is to take responsibility for having the various types of negative programming and to take steps to release ourselves from it. It is helpful for us to come to a realization of how having these types of negative programming, whether it be devices, entities, programs, replicators, dendrites, or implants, have served us. What gift did having these things as part of our being give us? How did they serve our ego? How has the pain we felt from this negative programming helped us?

We can use our muscle testing or our pendulums to help us to hone in on the answers to these questions. Coming to a place of understanding of why we allowed the creation of negative types of programming to come into our being sets the stage for us to track down the original lifetimes when they attached themselves to us; this helps us to clear them across all timelines and parallel realities.

We are victorious when we raise ourselves up in the love and light we are. We are victorious when we allow ourselves to feel the freedom of being in the Now moment connected in our heart centers to Creator-Source.

Letting Go of the Safe Place

Allowing ourselves to be in a safe place, where we felt the pain wouldn't get any worse and we knew what to expect, is more acceptable than making choices to bring us into new realms of experiencing our lives. It takes faith and trust to go into new situations when we don't have a firm grip on what to expect. When we take a jump into the unknown, we are allowing ourselves to grow in an exponential way. The level of confidence we can gain from succeeding to break out of our old routine can't be downplayed; it can be a springboard into reshaping our lives in a most beneficial way.

There are many ways that the dark forces have controlled us. One is the way they have contaminated our food supply and conditioned us to buy food that is a burden on our systems to process. There are many toxins in our food, such as refined sugar, preservatives, hormones, pesticides and herbicides, and genetically modified organisms. Things like gluten make our bodies work extra hard to digest it, and we become addicted to these things. Parasites and pathogens come into our body, and we feed them when we take in these toxins. It becomes an automatic response on our part to buy these things when we walk in the grocery store. Even though we know that we would have more energy by letting go of them, we hang onto them because it is a type of addiction, and they become our safe place. The choices we make to keep them become our safe choices, and other choices are perceived as unsafe.

We must use our power of intent to turn around this situation, where we have allowed ourselves to become the victims of the food industry. The food industry is linked hand in hand with the healthcare industry, and they are linked with the pharmaceutical companies to extract huge profits from us at the cost of our physical, emotional, mental, and spiritual bodies. After abusing our bodies with the toxins that contaminate our food, our bodies start to contract diseases, which benefit the healthcare industry when we use their types of insurance, western medical practitioners, and pharmaceutical drugs.

Some of us feel as if we must give our power away to a person who has a degree that says he or she knows more than us. Also, some of us feel that because the institutions to whom we have given permission to be the foundation of mainstream culture advocate only certain types of drugs, therapies, and practitioners, then we feel afraid to go against their advice.

It takes courage to realize that we are giving into fear and giving our power away to a money-making machine that doesn't have our best interests at heart; that in many instances, there are other choices for alternative care that are more in alignment with our sovereign being.

Some of us seek the refuge of being entertained or informed after we endure another hard day of work, coming home and turning on the TV or computer. This is when we are most susceptible to being taken over by the mind-control programming of the dark forces. This is when we are tired and in a passive state, which makes us susceptible to subliminal programming. Some of us have hard days at work and are already in a state of fear, running things inside our minds about the day we had and the problems that may seem overwhelming to us.

When we tell the universe that we want our bodies harmonized and balanced, that we will no longer give our power away to the food and healthcare industries; it is huge step that we take in empowering ourselves.

Using the Toolbox

It is our choice to use the tools we have to find new ways of handling the stresses in our daily routine. We can't rely only upon the mainstream media to inform us about what is really going on in our world anymore— they have shown themselves to be badly compromised by the dark forces. It is up to us to take the initiative and use our discernment to find other means of information. This may mean scouring the Internet for what resonates with us from a variety of sources, or it may mean watching videos that present the alternative side of things. It may mean trusting in the messages we receive in our dream states and in meditation.

It is only when we are willing to bust through the envelope of the same choices we have been making, which we realize aren't serving us anymore, that we begin to empower ourselves. This first step to make a change can be very unsettling for us. Perhaps we have had to allow ourselves to feel much pain and discomfort in adhering to our routines, before we took that first step to make a different choice. Maybe the concept that we can't keep making the same choices and expecting different results has finally gotten through to us.

All of us have a toolbox. One of the main things we find in it is the voice of our intuition. When we tap into and listen to it, we find we are able to send information to others psychically, to hear the thoughts of others, to know when something is going to happen or when someone is going to come into our reality, and to get downloads of information from the higher aspects of our being.

One of the main things in our toolbox is being able to trust our intuition or having confidence in the messages we receive. Muscle Response Testing is a great of way of confirming the guidance we receive from our intuition. I have heard some people say that learning how to trust their use of MRT was the most crucial thing for them in realizing self-empowerment.

A simple way to do MRT is to make circles by interlocking the thumb and pinky of each hand and placing them inside one another. We ask questions and program the response, so that if the answer is positive, the circles don't break when you try to break them, but if the answer is negative, the circles break apart.

You can also use a pendulum and program it to show a negative answer when the pendulum moves side to side. For a positive answer you can program your pendulum to move back and forth.

MRT is a practically infallible way for all of us to develop and monitor the accuracy of where our intuition is pointing us. You can become proficient with this tool by asking yourself questions you know the answers to and later having someone ask you questions that they know the answers to. You can use MRT in everyday life: when you're in a grocery store and you want to buy the best product, you can ask whether or not it is in your highest interest to buy it.

A big part of becoming proficient at using MRT for the clearings is listening to your intuition to know what questions to ask for guidance, for yourself or for your client. This means getting connected to Creator-Source in our heart centers and then listening to what comes through.

We will get promptings about what to ask, and so by using MRT or our pendulums, we narrow things down by getting yes and no answers to our questions, which helps us go in the direction of finding the answers we are after.

Meg used to say that you want to tug on the fear, that you want to go to the places where you or your client get disconnected from Creator-Source. This helps you to determine what program you are looking for, and then you test to see what lifetime in which it was first activated. We validate the messages or insights we are receiving by using MRT or pendulums when we see the results manifest in our reality. With this simple tool we can remove much of the doubt and fear from our lives. I have mostly used MRT, and I have felt much gratitude for having it in my life, because it has helped me to simplify making choices. It may take a while before you trust the answers you are getting, but when you do, it will help you trust your connection to Creator-Source, and this will be a profound blessing for you. MRT truly helps us to stay on course and to validate the choices we are making.

Patience is a magnificent tool that we possess. It takes practice to develop, and it is apparent to many others—and me—that we are being tested for how patient we can be in this lifetime. When all seems as if it isn't going our way, it takes courage, perseverance, inner strength, and great willpower to forge ahead. When we have patience and take things in stride, we allow ourselves to be in the Now moment and not lose sight of how we are divine, interdimensional beings of love and light, and the experience of being a human is a holographic illusion. It is a kindness we show to others and ourselves in being patient. It shows we have trust in Creator-Source that everything is in its right rhythm, timing, and synchronization.

Gratitude is also one of the most beneficial tools we have. When we allow ourselves to be grateful for all we have, it helps us be in the Now moment. When we have gratitude for the lessons we are learning through the experience of navigating the obstacles and challenges with which we are presented, we keep the connection with Creator-Source open, and gratitude strengthens our connection with Creator-Source. We uplift the energies we are working with, and our level of attraction is raised. We can be grateful for our ability to create and also uncreate. We acknowledge that all of creation is One.

Forgiveness is the ability to recognize we have caused ourselves pain by going for the illusion of separation between ourselves and Creator-Source. When we forgive ourselves for feeling this pain of separation, we own our creations and acknowledge we are never separate from the All That Is. This realization extends to others who help us co-create our experiences. We realize we must first forgive ourselves in order to forgive others for the role they played in helping us co-create what caused us the pain of separation.

Flexibility of our minds and emotions enables us to let go of fixed solutions to challenges. We must take into account that under the present condition of having the veil in place, we can't know how our actions will affect the whole. Often the reason we are being told to change our approach to handling the challenges in our life is that higher aspects of our being are testing us to see if we can trust in the guidance we are getting.

Having a balance between the male and female aspects of our being plays a big part in allowing us to be flexible and not go for fixed images. Nature contains free-flowing imagery, and the world of advertising contains fixed imagery. Which feels better? It is up to us to make choices in accordance with our true nature. Giving up the belief that the fixed images in our outer reality determine our own worth and self-esteem is integral in helping us be who we really are.

There is much societal and peer pressure upon us to act and think a certain way, but we must ask ourselves who is benefitting from it. We must push the envelope in which society wants to live. We are all conditioned to be good consumers. In much of Western culture, our consumption of products isn't beneficial to Mother Gaia—it benefits the big corporations who want to run our lives to keep their power over us.

Learning how to let go of whether we are right or wrong is one of the biggest challenges we face. We do this by being able to let go of the ego as the dominant force in our minds. When we are able to balance the mind with the heart, we can connect with the higher aspects of our being or the inner knowing we all possess. We come to accept we are all part of the whole, and each one of us has a role to play. It is when we respect one another for the part each of us plays that we can come together within the sanctuary of our hearts and make choices for the good of all.

We are all mirrors of one another, and we must accept that all of us have been playing this game of being a human on planet earth for a very long time, and that now our time in duality is coming to a close. We are poised for graduation day, which is our ascension or the acquisition of full consciousness, while we are still in human bodies on planet earth. It serves us well at this time to appreciate the roles others have played in our lives and to see that judgment against one another is a part of the programs initiated by the dark forces to separate us—it doesn't serve us. There is much power when we align with one another for the good of All That Is.

To know that all of creation is One is to know we are never against anyone or anything, that no one is against us, or that no one judges us. It is to understand all of us are just doing our jobs, playing out the roles we have given ourselves permission to play. It is to know that we are all the same in the light of love we have been created in, and we have chosen different tasks to do in this life. It is up to each of us to be responsible in asking for and receiving the help of the universe, and accepting that this may take various forms.

We can use our imaginations in a meditative state to go to higher dimensions and clear the polarities of war and greed in places all over Mother Gaia. We do this on our own or join in group meditations, either in person or remotely, to focus our love and light on these affected areas to cleanse them so that the old programs and karma from them can be healed, and the new higher vibrating energies can come in to harmonize with the blueprint of the new earth we are envisioning for this golden age of ascension.

When we are not in a meditative state, the creativity of our imagination is still a great tool for us to utilize. We can connect the dots between all of the information we have and bring the whole picture into focus for ourselves and others. How we do this is up to us; each of us are a unique ray of the creator's love, and by accessing the power of our intent, we can use the gift of imagination in our own distinctive way to create a flow, attracting the frequencies of love and light, which can help others and ourselves master the demands of playing this game of life. When we are in this place of flow or connection with the All That Is, our actions come to us effortlessly. We create by being moved or inspired and by following our divine guidance or intuition.

Sometimes it may mean singing a song, cracking a joke to break up tension, or telling a story. Whatever forms the expression of our creative imagination takes on, it becomes a great tool for connecting with Creator-Source and with others, to raise the level of consciousness.

Anytime we feel fear coming into the bodies of our being, we can shift gears with the power of our intent and go back to the zero point with our conscious breathing. When we do this, we let go of tension and allow ourselves to be of no thing and no mind; this is a place of higher consciousness and being who we truly are. From there we can start fresh and bring in the highest frequencies of love and light.

Love Is the Highest Vibrational Healing Tool

We are the victor when we allow and will ourselves to love. Love encompasses the vibrations of accepting, allowing, nurturing, faith, trust, and being in the Now moment, among other things. Love is the place of being One with the All That Is; it is the place of connection inside of our heart center with Creator-Source.

We are all in a grand experiment of raising the level of vibration. Over the course of these many lifetimes, we have played out many roles with one another. We have been cut off in the dark from knowing who we truly are, and now we are approaching a place where each of us is coming into our full light and full consciousness while still in this human incarnation.

We empower ourselves and all of creation when we see how the institutions of the dark have manipulated us into being slaves in their plan of dominating us and the planet, and when we allow ourselves to let go of all of the fear-based programming. It is up to us to learn how to forgive ourselves for the pain we have felt over feeling separated from Creator-Source. Then we are able to forgive all the others who played out their roles with us in this illusory holographic 3-D game of love and light.

It is now time for us to see each other for the love and light we are. When we join together with others who are awakening, we raise the level of our consciousness in an exponential way, accelerating the ascension process for us all. We can do this in meditations or various projects that spread our gifts and talents in creative, life-affirming ways.

It is up to us to eliminate the lower vibrations from our reality; by eliminating negative programming, we help ourselves and others to achieve this, bringing in more love and light. Now love and light are dominating the vibrations of our existence on this planet; this higher level of consciousness helps us to rise up and exponentially advance the ascension process for the planet, others, and ourselves.

Each time we send our love outward into the All That Is, we raise the level of the vibration. We are at the tipping point of taking us firmly out of the Iron Age and into the Golden Age of our ascension. It is our choice to be here at this time when we are bringing the testing of the game of duality to a close. The lower vibrations won't hold any sway over us to perpetuate the illusion of separation. Now is our time of being victorious in our mission and purpose, of being in full consciousness while still incarnated.

PART TWO

Chapter 1

Core Fear Matrix Removal Program

Adapted by Dr. Margaret (Meg) Hoopes

What is a core fear matrix? Your body remembers and stores in cellular memory both what you and others say to it as well as what it experiences with all attending emotions. This is said to be the imprinting process, which begins when we are conceived and intensifies in the womb when our nervous systems are developed in the sixth month of gestation.

Two dominant emotions shape our experience: love and fear. Fear has been the dominant underlying emotion on our planet, since our advent into duality about 13,000 years ago. Any feeling that is not love is embedded in fear. Another way of saying this is that there are only two ways of thinking: with your Christ-like mind or with your negative-ego mind. (You don't have to be a Christian to have a Christ-like mind. Everyone is born with a Christ within.) A core fear is deep rooted and has many parts, such as a web, a matrix, or a root system.

Because of the core fear matrices that we carry, our spiritual evolution is hampered. To assist us in removing fear from our lives, the Spiritual Hierarchy2*, released the core fear matrix removal program for humanity. This is a marvelous gift! (For reference, see the book *Soul Psychology* by Joshua David Stone.)

This program can be used by an individual or in a group setting. I use it for myself constantly and in sessions with individuals, couples, and families, because many fears are common to individuals. I do group fear releases. I also combine emotional body cleansing with the fear removal program for excellent, lasting results. To use it personally or with others, you can refer to the outline of the core fear matrix release provided later in this chapter. Many of us need someone to take us through the removal when we are immersed in our negative emotions or in denial of them. You can reach us by e-mail if you have any questions. Please look at the end of this manual where we have our contact list.

It will help you to put the outline of the core fear matrix removal on a card and carry it with you until it becomes a "golden habit." This will allow you to be more at ease, because you won't be concerned about what to say next.

The Spiritual Hierarchy will actually pull your fear patterns right out of your subconscious mind and your four-body system (physical, emotional, mental, and spiritual) up through your crown chakra; they are permanently removed from your cell memory and from your soul records. Clairvoyantly these can be seen as black roots with tentacles throughout your being, and you may feel this process as energy moving up your body and out the crown of your head or another part of the body. Some feel it leave through the solar plexus; some people don't feel anything. A common feeling is one of wiggly energy in the brain.

The first thing to do is to choose the spiritual team that will remove the core fears matrices. The first member of the team is your mighty "I Am" presence (the Holy Spirit, essence, or whatever you call that presence within yourself.) Then select two members of the Spiritual Hierarchy. These two beings will be ascended masters who will help to co-ordinate the clearing with our "I Am" presence.

Two of the Spiritual Hierarchy, Vywamus and Djwhal Kuhl, brought this program to us through Joshua David Stone. When choosing those in the spiritual planes to help you, Stone suggests that you select those at the "ray" level or above. The Earth has benefited from seven rays coming from the Creator-Source to help us in our journeys.

Here is a list of masters associated with the twelve rays. Please note that these masters have other assignments too.

The Twelve Rays of Light

Chaneled from Mahachohan Saint Germain by Natalie Glasson 10-29-08

I am Saint Germain the Mahachohan; this means that I assist the Planetary Logos Lord Buddha in overseeing the mission and purpose of the Rays of light. I predominantly oversee the third ray of light, which is focused on manifestation. The third ray of light assists all twelve rays of light in materializing and anchoring into the Earth. It is for this reason that I supervise the rays three to seven as these are most needed on the Earth currently and are extensions of the third ray of light.

Each ray of light extends from the Creator's mighty soul through the universe and anchors into the planetary level of the Creator's universe. A ray of light holds its own special vibrations and colors expressing certain valued sacred qualities of the Creator's soul. I wish to share the main principles of the twelve rays of light to begin to clear all false beliefs and false information that is circulated. People have connected to and understood the rays of light for many years, channels have brought through the meanings of the rays and the masters connected to them to help others evolve and experience the rays. Many are forgetting that as the Earth and humanity grow and evolve so do the rays of light and their chohans.

Especially in this current time many masters are occupying the positions of chohan or governor of the rays for a limited amount of time as they are evolving to new positions to allow others to learn and grow with the

59

assistance of the rays of light. Many people continue to use information that was given years ago as their guide to connecting with the rays, this is fine but much has occurred since. As time doesn't exist on the inner planes people on the Earth can still connect with the past chohans and draw on the energies of the rays of light but it is important for you to focus on connecting with the new energies and higher vibrations of the rays that are available in our modern day.

It is important for all to remember that the rays of light have become stronger than ever before; they are integrating deeply as one as are their chohans, which is making it increasingly difficult to distinguish which master is overseeing which ray of light. Many are working with several rays of light. I hope that you will accept with an open heart and mind the enlightenment that I now wish to share with you all on the Earth.

I wish to now reveal to you my perception of the rays as they are from this date, 29-10-08.

Main Rays of Light

1st Ray—Red

Governed by Master El Morya and overseen by the Manu Allah Gobi

At lower levels it anchors from the Creator's soul courage, confidence, inner power, bravery, passion, driving force and enthusiasm. On a higher level it integrates the will and divine plan of the Creator.

2nd Ray—Blue

Governed by Master Joshua and overseen by the Christ Lord Maitreya.

Anchors the wisdom of the Creator through the embodiment of love, prepares souls for the acceptance of the Christ consciousness. The second ray of light is acknowledged as a special spiritual school that instigates spiritual development.

3rd Ray—Yellow

Governed by Master Serapis Bey and overseen by the Mahachohan Saint Germain

Anchors the ability to manifest through the power of the mind, aids mastery and clarity of the mind while assisting in the expression of love through thought forms to manifest the energy of the Creator on the Earth.

Extension Rays of Light

4th Ray—Green

Governed by Master Paul the Venetian and overseen by the Mahachohan Saint Germain

Anchors the energy of peace, tranquility, balance and harmony. Assists in accessing creative artistic abilities and expressing the soul in a creative way to reveal inner beauty. It can act as a cleansing ray restoring harmony within beings and in realities.

5th Ray—Orange

Governed by Master Hilarion and overseen by the Mahachohan Saint Germain

It is a key energy in the ascension and spiritual growth process of soul activation and soul discovery. At a lower level it aids projects of discovery or scientific developments. At a higher level it focuses predominantly on the soul's integration with the person's reality and with their personality on the Earth.

6th Ray—Indigo

Governed by Master Lanto and overseen by the Mahachohan Saint Germain

This ray of light is one of the purest forms of devotion and acceptance of the Creator's soul within your reality. It is an inspirational energy boost that aids deeper connections and understanding of the Creator's soul and universe. It explores the definition of devotion and how to exist as a devoted light being to the mighty soul of the Creator while accepting one's own inner powers.

7th Ray—Violet

Governed by Lady Portia and overseen by the Mahachohan Saint Germain

This is the home of the violet flame of transmutation. It is also an essential energy on the Earth as it raises consciousnesses and anchors a new age of awareness into minds with higher vibrations. It is known as the awakening ray of light that assists in connecting with the higher rays of light.

The Higher Rays of Light

8th Ray—Sea Foam Green

Governed by Lady Nada and overseen by the Divine Director of the Rays

This is the deep spiritual cleansing ray that assists with preparations for soul activation and discovery. Healing and cleansing is always needed to access new vibrations and consciousnesses and can be gained from the eighth ray ashram.

9th Ray—Blue Green

Governed by Lady Mary and overseen by the Divine Director of the Rays

This ray holds a wealth of knowledge that can be grasped to aid soul discovery and expansion. It focuses on anchoring joy which is an expression of love while promoting integration on new levels with the energy of the Creator's soul and universe.

10th Ray—Pearlescent

Governed by Lady Master Andromeda and overseen by the Divine Director of the Rays.

This is ray promotes and instigates soul integration, monad integration and unity with the Creator's mighty soul.

11th Ray—Pink Orange

Governed by Lady Quan Yin and overseen by the Divine Director of the Rays

Again associates with soul discovery and integration, as are all the higher rays, this ray completes the soul merge process. It promotes an understanding that everything in the universe is a manifestation of love. It is a place where the teachings of all previous rays are integrated to aid an understanding and acceptance of mastery that is complete, allowing the soul to fully embody the higher ray of the Creator's universe including the twelfth ray of light.

12th Ray—Golden

Governed by Pallas Athena and overseen by the Divine Director of the Rays and Lord Maitreya.

The twelfth ray of light holds a direct link to the Office of the Christ and acts as a teaching ground for those wishing to embody the Christ consciousness. The twelfth ray of light is an extension of the Office of the Christ and anchors the loving energy of the Creator into all rays of light and throughout the Creator's universe especially the Earth.

I am the Mahachohan Saint Germain.

Reprinted with kind permission by Natalie Glasson www.omna.org

If none of these ascended masters resonate with you, you can call on those in your own belief systems. Be sure that you use your "I Am" presence or however you address the spirit within you. Those working with North American Indian traditions call on the ones with whom they are working. We will help you with names to fit your belief system and work with you to find the right combination for you.

Be alert for clues, such as negative emotions. Fear is always attached, so immediately ask for its removal. As the clearing continues, your choices will be clear and in alignment with your spiritual progression. This program works if you make the request. Your request can be comprehensive to fit your belief system.

Core Fear Matrix Removal Procedures

Example: List of Fears

Fear of not being able to heal my teeth and having to go to the dentist.

Fear of being in a car accident.

Fear of running out of money.

Fear of wasting time (i.e., not being productive and efficient).

Fear of not finding a job.

Fear of being abandoned and cut off from people.

Fear of making mistakes.

Fear of not doing the right thing.

Fear of not listening to my intuition.

Fear of going insane.

Fear of being cheated.

Fear of being judged and rejected by others.

Fear of being wrong.

Fear of having my ego take over my mind.

Fear of not knowing what choices to make.

Fear that my car will break down.

Fear that I've wasted my only opportunities to liberate myself.

Fear of the unknown fear.

Fear of loss:

- Loss of self, the greatest loss of all (with grief and sadness associated with it).

- Loss of life, family, looks, youth, agility, endurance, memory, friends, sight.

- Loss of control of one's life, money, home, job, freedom, talents, resilience, hope.

- Loss of faith, love, laughter, humor, self-reliability, courage, sense of direction, adaptability, intention, attention, spiritual gifts.

Core Fear Matrix Removal Program Outline—Meg Hoopes

1. Identify the fears you wish to release. It helps to write them down. The first time, make a list of twenty fears. All feelings and emotions that are not love are based in fear frequencies. Include fear of forgiveness and fear of

the unknown fear. You can put your hand on your list or direct energy to it, depending on whether it is on paper or on your computer screen.

2. Identify and call forth your team: your "I Am" presence and two ascended masters. You may use the same ones Meg used (Vywamus and Djwal Kuhl), or you may use the other ascended masters of the twelve rays listed above, or you may have other preferences. Whomever you choose forms a very powerful triangle of energies. As you call this team forth, notice the loving energy that comes in and around you. By clearing the core fear matrices from the four bodies of your being you also bless the planet. Therefore, it is a joyous service for your team.

3. Speak the request out loud or in your mind.

    Example: "Beloved I Am presence, Vywamus and Djwal Kuhl, please remove the core fear matrix attached to the list of twenty fears and all of the patterns attached to these fears."

4. From where do you want the fears to be released?

    "Release these fears and patterns from all of my bodies in my present life, from all aspects of myself, from all dimensions known and unknown, from all incarnations across space and time, from my genetic lineage, from my spiritual lineage, from all parallel and alternate realities, from all parallel and alternate universes, from all planetary systems, from all source systems, and from all places where these fears and patterns may be that we have not mentioned."

5. Ask for assistance from the medical teams from the medical ship the *Phoenix,* hovering in our outer atmosphere.

"I call for the medical teams from the *Phoenix* to come forth and release all of the following connected to the identified fears and patterns: structures, devices, machines, entities, parasites, orientations, crystals, suction cups, hidden micro chips; antennas not of my bodies, entities and/or their effects, all etheric imprints from death and torture devices, all etheric wounds from these devices and other death devices such as bullets, knives, hanging, swords, arrows and clubs. I call for all available healing energies to enter and surround my bodies in my parallel lives, thereby assisting the medical teams. I ask for restoration of perfection with balance and harmony in all of my bodies and places where these fears and patterns have been removed."

6. This begins the clearing and may take as long as three days to complete or much less time than this, and you can muscle test for how long it will take.

   "Thank you, teams! I give you my love and blessings!"

7. We now call in the clean-up crew, angel power!

   "Beloved Blue Angels with the blazing blue swords, come forth and cut all attachments between the fears and patterns and all persons, places, conditions, and things in my being and world."

   "Beloved Violet Angels, come forth and blaze the violet consuming flame up through my feet and into every cell in my body, consuming all disqualified and discredited energy, and all cell memory the memory of the memory and habits and memory of the habits attached to these fears and patterns."

8. Praise and gratitude lifts us up and connects us to spirit and the cosmic beings. We can't overdo blessing, praising, and thanking our assistants.

9. Forgiveness is very important and must come from our heart center with deliberate intent. When you are ready, place one or both hands over your heart center.

    "Beloved I Am presence, I call forth the law of forgiveness, I call forth the law of mercy, I call forth the love from deep within my heart center. I forgive myself and all others who helped me co-create these fears and patterns."

    Pause and notice any resistance. You may have to do a fear release related to forgiveness. If you are not satisfied that it has cleared, do the forgiveness again. You can also do the Ho O Pono Pono, which translates into English as, "I'm sorry, please forgive me, thank you, I love you."

10. You have just experienced a powerful removal of energy from your bodies, due to the power of love. Replace all cell memory and patterns of fear with love by making the following request:

    "Beloved I Am presence, pour through the crown of my head your gold and white light, cleansing, purifying, beautifying, sanctifying, and increasing the light in every cell, thereby rewriting cellular memory with love and giving me an ever-expanding capacity to love myself, others, the planet and all that live in her, on her, and above her, and the universe. Give me an ever-expanding capacity to accept love from myself, from others, from the Planet and all that live in her, on her and above her, the universe, and the void. So be it! So it is!"

    We can ask our higher self how long it will take for the clearing to be completed. Our teams will continue to work on us until all of the clearing has been done.

Exercise to Thank Fear for Its Lessons

This excerpt is from *Principles and Applications of the
Twelve Universal Laws:* A Workbook for Children of All Ages

Written and Illustrated by Leia A. Stinnett

Sit quietly and take a few deep breaths. Let your mind settle on your heart center. Create a crystal-clear flame. See this flame contained within a tube in the center of your body. Within this tube create a spiral of crystal-clear liquid light moving clockwise. Create a second spiral of crystal-clear liquid light moving counter clockwise. The liquid light spirals up and down and in and out at the same time. Feel the spirals of light moving up and down and in and out. You do not have to see them.

Move the spirals up and down until you feel a deeper connection to God. Find that place in the energy of God that is your special space. You came from God and there is one special place within God's loving energy that is for you and you alone.

Feel the love of Creator-Source. Make the love stronger and stronger until all you feel is this love.

Let one of your biggest fears come into your consciousness. Think about it. Face your fear. Focus all of your attention on the fear. As you look at the fear, what lessons are you learning from the experience? Is the fear teaching you to stand in your own power? To not listen to other people? To make your own decisions? To change what you do not like with your own power to create with Creator-Source whatever you choose? Is the fear related to something that happened in a past life?

As you recognize the lesson to be learned, the fear begins to lessen and disappear in the spirals of light. Thank the fear for teaching you what you have asked to learn. Acknowledge that the fear no longer serves you in this life experience. Forgive yourself for being afraid, and lovingly release the fear into the spiral of light, where the fear will immediately be transmuted into God's loving light. God's very own "recycling center" will change the old fear energy into new positive, loving energy that can be used again and again.

Anytime you feel afraid, stop whatever you are doing. Create the spirals of liquid light. Release your fear with love. The sooner you release the fear, the less energy you will have time to give it and the easier it will be for you to remain in a loving space.

The Quickie Fear Release

Dr. Margaret (Meg) Hoopes

12/28/09

Introduction

A major part of spirited clearings is to get rid of fears. The core fear matrix release deals with fears attached to a matrix holding fears from many lifetimes and connecting and affecting our present lives. The quickie fear release clears fears we are feeling connected to a situation in our present life. Perhaps you have a new job or task, and you fear you cannot do it. You may receive a notice in the mail that your bills are going to a collection agency, or you meet someone from your past who frightens you. Someone is confronting you, blaming you for something you did or did not do. The examples are endless, but the quickie fear release can help them all.

Recognition

Recognize you are afraid and begin exploring it. "I am afraid that . . ." You usually know, but if you don't, just call it "this fear" or "these fears." Where is this fear? It is in your etheric body and affecting your emotions, your physical body, and your thinking. Own that you have the power and knowledge to get rid of it.

Position and Tools

Sit with your feet on the floor, in a chair in which you are able to lean forward. (Or you may stand.) Your powerful tools are your hands and fingers. Open your hands and hold them in front of you. Look at the center of your palms and know and own the power of the energy center (chakra). You have used it many times to smooth away tension in a part of your body, such as when you hold a baby and rub her back. What a wonderful gift it is! Look at the ends of your fingers and thumbs, and know that you also have powerful charkas there.

You often direct that energy at others with laser quality without conscious intent. I was in a laser Reiki class, talking to students when the class was having a break, I casually pointed my finger at someone in what I would call a natural gesture and made a statement. I was not confronting anyone. He said, "Ouch—you have no idea how powerful that laser shot was you just gave me." That opened my understanding. I realized I had a powerful tool, and I must be careful, and that my intentions in using it must be pure.

Procedures

1. Look down between your feet and imagine an opening into the earth, like a coal chute. You can make it a color so that is distinctive. (Mine is red.) It is going to receive your fears, and the earth will neutralize them.

2. Now using the palms of your hands and your fingers and thumbs, reach above your head and pull the fears from that part of your etheric body (your aura) and pull them down and around to the front of your body. Place the fear energy in your solar plexus, your third charka. Now collect the fear energy from your shoulders and back, depositing them in the third charka. Systematically move down your body collecting and depositing the fear energy from all parts of your body, including the bottoms of your feet. With clear intention and attention, this process does not take very long.

3. With your hands, collect some of the energy from the third charka and push it down through the second charka, through the root charka, and into the chute between your feet. I put a "whooshing" sound with it, giving it more force. Continue with this procedure until all energy in the third charka is now in the chute, going, going, gone. Allow yourself to feel the releases. You may ask if it is all gone, and you will receive an answer. Move your feet together to close the chute.

4. Thank the fear for what it has taught you. Do forgiveness for yourself and others, and praise and bless yourself and others. Don't forget to thank Mother Earth.

5. It doesn't matter when you do the step of negative dendrite removal. This can be added by doing a negative program removal at any time.

You will get so good at this that you can think your way through it in the company of others, and they won't know what you are doing. After the release, they may respond to you differently, more positively.

CHAPTER 2

Removal of Handlers Blocking Particular Healings

Taken from the Channel of Ashtar, through Susan Leland
Household and Hovering Handlers

The handlers (controllers) are trained by the Illuminati to influence mortals to actions and feelings that upset their harmony and balance and, through them, the harmony and balance of those people around them.

Hovering handlers love malls, cults, and places where people who gather there are somewhat fanatical. The hovering handlers roam and zero in where they see a weakness. They tend to travel in packs where there is famine, war, and genocide. They love to go to prison. They don't have a program of who they attach to, to target any one specific individual. They are considered to be more powerful, because they don't choose who they are attached to.

When a human being is infected by a handler, and he or she decides to come to the light, the energy of the hoverer is released. To clear the handlers out of the circle of beings they may be hovering around, we need to clear them out of the atmosphere. The goal is transmutation. Some light workers have a tendency to release the negative energy they are feeling from the handlers. They throw out the energy into the universe, where it comes back like a boomerang in the form of hovering handlers or household handlers, depending on what they were before.

When we do a clearing on a person who has had handlers, and we release them, it is necessary to transmute the energy of the handlers. Many people believe that if they say, "Be gone forevermore" and put the white light around them or use some other ritual or technique, then the hovering or household handlers can't come back to them. What these people are really doing is sending the handlers out of their bodies, but the handlers have no place to go. They become loose and the fly around as hovering handlers, looking for other people to jump into and take over.

Are they evil? No. They have been programmed to do evil. They are just energies, whether they are residing in a body or not. These energies are the handlers of the handlers, and they are being removed. We have been working to clear them for some time now, and their removal is coming along very nicely. It is simply up to us to do some cleanup. We just wanted you to understand that the energies of handlers are waiting to inhabit bodies that have low vibrations. They are just outside of your energy fields.

Now, you might say energy fields are kind of mixed in with each other, so if we clear them out of a being's energy field, why can't we get them to be removed that way? There is such a thing as separate and apart, even though it might seem as though it is all one. And so it is from the atmosphere that you are actually asked to do the clearings, rather than from a specific group or population of beings. We clear the energy fields first through the individual, because the handlers are rooted there, but the energy of the handlers extends into the atmosphere. The atmosphere needs to be cleared to remove & transmute the energy of the handlers totally.

Very infrequently they will attach to animals, and they may cause an animal that has been friendly to become unfriendly for no apparent reason, when there is nothing that can be recognized in the animal's physicality. You might see or sense that there is a handler energy there that got a little off target, because they are not generally here to concern themselves with the animal kingdom. But if for instance a doggy who has been friendly to you starts to snarl at your approach, that doggy may have been actually attached to a handler or may be telling you that there is some being in your atmosphere who is trying to attach or is attached to you.

Pay attention and get the message, asking for clarity. Clarification always works, and you can always fall back upon your testing. That is just another little line we thought we would include here. We would like to be all inclusive about this topic, because there are many things that you are going to go on to do, to support all of the healings, the technologies, the techniques, and the self-acknowledgments that will come as people start waking up to the fact that they have all of the power they need to play their part in this mass awakening of humanity and the planet. You are going to be here to teach and support people who want to wake up and take back the power they have given away when they were taken over by these dark programs. There will be a day soon when the handler energies will be totally clean from the planet, and until then we ask you to continue with clearing the negative programs as they also encompass clearing handler programming.

As you dig deeper, you discover more and more webs of fear programming to remove, and you will be supporting the housecleaning in the area of removing handlers as well. There will be some other exercises that will come to light as you proceed. And we shall be partying too, because you know it is a grand gift to others and yourself when you party: you lift up, you are in joy, and you radiate it outward. With all these things that are available to you, we might say that you were standing at the smorgasbord of delightful adventures and service to the world and the universe beyond, so power up and go for it.

We're with you in all that you do. We are love expressed to you, and we thrive and nurture ourselves upon the love that you express to us—never doubt it. And so I, Ashtar, have completed the message that I have been so delighted to give.

We shall at this moment say thank you, beloveds; we are so much in love with you. You are so dear to us and have so many reigning colors of service that we can't even count them, and there is really no need, is there? And on that note, we shall say thank you for being here in this sacred space to do this sacred mission. Until we meet again in the formality of the podium, remember we are here, we're there, we're everywhere, and so it is. Salut.

CHAPTER 3

Negative Program Removals

Recognition of Dendrites

2/10/09

Summary Guide

Meg Hoopes

(Editor's note: As time went on, it became apparent that the negative dendrites were a big part of negative programs. So while I feel it is very helpful for us to understand the function of dendrites and the part they play, I have come to think of them as part of the negative programs and do not clear them separately. Toward the end of her life, Meg comprised many components of the fear programming, such as negative dendrites, curses, vows, dogmas, into the negative program removals in order to clear them completely and thoroughly at one time.)

Introduction and Purpose

What are dendrites, and why are they important now in our evolution? The dendrites and their neuronets form a web of connections and information. They are part of the structure of our brains—a very busy part. We could liken them to memory chips recording all that happens to us in our four bodies, physical, emotional, mental, and spiritual. Recently I heard part of a discussion about brain activity on National Public Radio. It is estimated that there are more than eight billion magnetic electronic contact points in the brain. Every second one of those points can fire more than three thousand times. Dendrites store our memories and the history of our experiences in this lifetime, as well as remnants from other lifetimes.

Many of these dendrites are dormant, and some of them are very active as we live our daily experiences. Those that store negative energy need to be released from our bodies. When we release and transmute negative energy, we are cleansing our bodies and Mother Earth. Her body sighs with pleasure with the release, as do our bodies.

Learn to be dendrite sensitive. We get signals from one of the bodies of our being when a negative dendrite is activated. For example, we feel pain in our physical body or sometimes the brain activates uncomfortable feelings. Thoughts and emotions signal activation of dendrites, and a memory picture may flash in our brains. Our habitual response may be to rationalize it or ignore it. A dendrite may be connected to such things as vows, beliefs, dogma, family and personal stories, betrayals, lies, behavioral actions, and smells—all which comprise negative programs. When a negative dendrite is activated, our spirit and guides will nudge us in directions we can go to release and clear it.

What is your intention? Is it to become dendrite sensitive? Is it to participate in this method to assist in your cleansing process, and thereby assist in bringing harmony and balance to this planet?

The dendrites are an important part of clearing negative programs. We clear them when we are doing a negative program removal. You will be asking questions about the negative programs and the direction to move in the process of determining what the originating lifetime of the negative program was. This will enable you to co-create the clearing in all lifetimes and timelines. Use MRT, a pendulum, or your knowingness, or have someone else test you on the questions you have.

For example, to move through the process I will use a statement" "Well, I won't hold my breath until that happens." This statement could mean a lack of trust, expecting others to make the reality for you, not believing that what you have asked for has already been given to you, ingratitude for all you have in this Now moment, denying that everything in the universe is in divine timing, or not knowing and appreciating that you have everything you need inside of you. Ask them how many times they have said or thought that or heard someone say it. The question is meant to stimulate a feeling with them. You are searching for where fear is active within them. If this statement doesn't work for you, identify one that will.

When you get them to reveal where they are afraid, it may bring up other issues that need clearing. It is with your pure intent, discernment, and patience that you will help your client or yourself put together the pieces of what you are dealing with to determine what negative program would be in the best interest to clear in this Now moment.

Removal of Negative Programs and Replicators

Meg Hoopes

Revised 11/25/09

Introduction

Negative programs are the creation of the Illuminati scientists. The intention of the programs is to keep the individual frightened, off balance, and cut off from the positive energies such as love, joy, and good health. From experience the Illuminati scientists knew that humans would find ways to remove and neutralize the programs. Numerous students told me in my teleconference class that they were doing the clearings continuously, but the symptoms would come back. In sessions on the telephone I received the same message from experienced light workers and healers.

My students are my teachers, so I paid attention. In a telephone session we would remove a program, and in a few moments it would come back. I asked my guides, my masters, and my higher self for an answer. I was given the word "replicator" and an understanding of a very clever backup action. When a program is removed by an individual or individuals, the replicator activates a mirror image of the program. I have been told many times by those who guide me from higher dimensions, "If you can think it, you can do it." With that belief in action, I put together a way to remove and dismantle the program and disable the replicator.

I asked Mother Sekhmet and her team to find the negative programs and disable the replicators before taking out the program. We asked them to search out the other active negative programs and clear them and their replicators. I then asked Archangel Amethyst to come with her legion of the violet flame angels to clear all negative residual energies of the programs. I found out later that many others from other dimensions were involved, including the Z'or Continuum angels.

I later worked with my bodies. By identifying symptoms that reoccur or never completely heal, I found that my bodies (physical, emotional, mental, and spiritual) contained many negative programs and their replicators. Although the team had removed many programs, I looked for programs to be layered and found that to be true. This is consistent with our findings with other spirited clearings. We are clearing all other lifetimes, and the negative programs are layered, so it may take many times and many helpers to completely clear them. With so many of us awakening and taking an active part in raising the level of consciousness with these clearings, it becomes a simpler task to clear them.

The removal of these negative programs can be done remotely. We never gave permission to have these programs in us, so we do not need to have permission to remove them. If you feel guided to clear negative programs from someone, you don't need their permission to do it remotely.

In some cases torture and disease, such as cancer, were used to create a condition of extreme pain. This condition was held in place and time by dendrites, curses, vows, dogmas, and handlers. The reason why we don't clear a negative program just in this lifetime is because it is contained in the lifetime it was originally contracted in, and it may also be in a parallel reality or timeline.

By doing muscle testing to find the original lifetime where the condition we want to clear exists, we ask questions to remove the web of related dendrites, handlers, and curses, which are invariably part of a negative program, of which replicators are also active.

Identification of Healings

When I am working with clients, I ask them what is reoccurring in their life that they would like to release. The answers range from the physical, mental, and emotional issues they are going through. When we get three or four issues, I ask my team which one is in the best interest of the other people or myself to clear at this time. Sometimes I ask that more than one program be cleared from the same originating lifetime. During the session I may decide to clear other programs that don't have the same originating lifetime, but then I repeat the process of the Mother Sekhmet Healing for everytime I clear programs from an originating lifetime.

- These procedures can be utilized in distant healings, with or without the client's involvement. We never gave permission to have these programs in us, so we do not need to have permission to remove them. The removal does require a human working with those from higher dimensions.

- You may be experiencing the same symptoms as you did before you did an Illuminati negative program removal. This happened to me: I asked if I was dealing with an Illuminati negative program and got no answer. Then I was prompted to ask if I was dealing with a negative program co-created by some other source. I received a yes answer. "Who?" I asked. "You!" I received. I verified the answer and began a search for how to remove it.

Process

Recognition

Some people have a headache they can't get rid of. Some people have asthma. Pain comes from the physical body. All physical symptoms have thought patterns that go with them. Some people have what we call blocks and can't move forward on projects. The block is centered in the mental body, but it is often layered with fear, which is in the emotional body.

Your bodies—physical, emotional, mental, and spiritual—send you signals indicating activation of a negative program with negative energy, such as a sharp pain, a dull ache, confusion, apathy, a bad dream, anger, rage, rejection, low esteem, and hatred. As you become more sensitive to negative programs and their components, you will recognize the activity in yourself and others. Also, addictions of any type will have negative programs that need to be cleared.

Sometimes while you are doing the process of negative program removal, fear may be present and even intense enough that you will recognize it. Use your testing ability for clarification. You will want to use the exercise to thank fear for its lessons or the core fear matrix removal for this fear you are feeling.

Many of you think you have lost your hope, faith, or charity, believing you are doomed and that there is someone or something against you. There are archangels named Faith, Hope, and Charity who have gifted you with permanence in having faith, hope, and charity. They lie constantly in your heart-soul area and will help you to empower yourself and clear negative programs, entities, devices, and implants.

Use your pendulum, muscle response testing, dowsing, or knowingness to find out what program is in the highest good of yourself (or the person you are working on) to clear in this session. I use MRT because you need no equipment, only your fingers, muscles, and practice. You can validate your answers to gain confidence in yourself with it. MRT is highly scientific; refer to the book *Power Vs. Force*, by Stephen Hawkins.

Identification

We will use an example. You recognize that you have a headache. Rather than reaching for a headache remedy pill, ask, "Do I have a negative program active within me now?" Check the answer with muscle response testing or a pendulum. If yes, then you can go on with this process of gaining information about the negative programs.

a.   When you are first working with a person, it is helpful to identify a few of the issues that keep coming up with the person and determine what programs need to be cleared. I will come up with a list of what I feel needs to be cleared by asking the person what is causing them pain, what is causing them to feel life is hopeless and helpless, so they can create a better feeling life.

b.   When I determine which program I will be clearing, I will ask if this negative program is in this life and parallel lives. If I get yes to both questions, then I can start asking questions to pinpoint in which lifetime the negative program originated.

c.   I test to find out what was happening in the person's lifetime. I ask how many lifetimes on earth did this person have when this program originated, and then I test for a number to come up. You can continue asking questions by listening to your knowingness. Use MRT or use a pendulum until you get an understanding of what developed the negative program. I do this because the same patterns will be evident in the person's present lifetime to a varying degree. It is helpful to identify the pattern in this lifetime; it will give the person a better understanding of what has been going on, because this negative program has been active. Then you can ask if all the questions have been asked about this negative program. If you get a yes, you can move on to the removal process.

d. It will help you to keep a log or the clearings you have done with your clients, especially if you are doing more than one clearing with them. The log can be very simple:

Name of person and date of clearing

Name of the program: pressure over having to please others (bosses)

Has had 67 lifetimes on Earth

He was an administrative priest in the high temple in Lemuria. He began to feel pressure from the expectations of others. There was pressure from women over their healings or the healings of their children. He went for the manipulations of others who wanted him to do things their way. He felt that it was necessary for him to do this in order to keep his position. His bosses put pressure on him to please his clients.

Negative Entities

Some of us are or have been possessed by negative entities. I have noticed that some people who don't seem to make any progress when they try to clear the negative programming in their lives are possessed by entities. It seems as if they are trapped in a loop and keep playing out the same patterns of fear that cause them to react the same way time and time again.

Even though people don't want negative results, they keep on expecting that the same thoughts, words, and actions will bring them different results. It seems as if somewhere in their being, they keep on getting tricked by their egos, and because of fear they make the same choices that don't let them complete their plan of liberating themselves. After a while some of these people are too afraid to make different choices; they feel as if they are doomed and nothing will help them.

People who have been soldiers, worked in pornography, and have been addicted to substances or alcohol seem to be the most susceptible to being taken over by negative entities. Some of these negative beings are disembodied spirits who have lost their way to the other side. They want another body so they can play out their fears and addiction, but they can only climb into someone who is unconscious in the lower vibrations. Many of them died suddenly and weren't prepared for letting go of their bodies. They are afraid to cross over, so they feed off the fear of others once they find a body to hide in.

Some of the negative entities have been programmed to promote the darkness of the underworld. These types of negative entities— disembodied spirits and negative entities of the spirit underworld—have guilt, shame, terror, horror, hopelessness, grief, rage, and denial. All of these are stored in the brain along with dogmas, vows, and curses. The negative entities feed off of these emotions and beliefs, and they help perpetuate them within the person in which they reside.

Anytime we are in the lower vibrations, we aren't conscious of who we truly are, and this state of being paves the way for the handlers to come in. Fear is the total disconnect they are looking to activate within us. When they do, our connection to Creator-Source has been severed until we manage to rebuild it again; this enables the handlers to come in and bring a negative entity with them.

We can think of the negative handlers as the agents or catalysts who enable the negative entities to transition inside of us. These entities are part of the negative programs that the handlers are looking to install within us. They can't reside inside of us if we co-create their removal with our teams of angels and guides.

It is necessary that we go through the same steps of calling in our help to protect us with their energies when we do these clearings. Along with the beings of light that are in the text of the negative program removal, I, Eli, like to call in all of the ascended masters, archangels, blue angels, lavender angels, golden angels and violet flame angels, and any other celestial beings I, or my client, feels close to. It is enough for our teams to know our intent, and they will find the ways to do the work of ridding negative programs from our being.

Negative Program Removal

This modified procedure for clearing the negative programs below was channeled through one of Meg's students. This version of the removal is reflective of how the level of the vibrations of love and light have been raised on this planet since Meg started doing her work with these removals, combined with the efforts of all those light workers who have been raising the level of conscious awareness for so many years now.

There aren't as many steps to do to align with our teams, because they are more in synch with us and us with them. The bridges have been crossed and the trails have been blazed. The light is gaining in strength and dominance over the dark every day. The forward momentum is with us.

Mother Sekhmet Healing

A Modified Version of Meg Hoopes' Removal of Negative Programs and Replicators

We thank Beloved Mother-Father God for their divine protection. We now invoke the assistance of the highest realms of illumined truth and love:

- The Office of the Christ.

- My Divine I Am Presence.

- The Divine I Am presence of _____.

- Our Beloved guides and angels.

- Beloved Archangel Amethyst and the Angels of the Violet flame.

- Beloved Archangel Michael and his team of Angels with the Blazing Blue Swords.

- Beloved Guido of the Light and his team of angels.

- The Beloved Monitors.

- The Beloved Lavender Angels.

- Beloved Meg Hoopes.

We Now call forth Beloved Mother Sekhmet. Beloved Mother Sekhmet. Beloved Mother Sekhmet.

1. We ask Beloved Mother Sekhmet and her team to locate and remove all negative programs, handler programs, negative entities, negative dendrites, and disruptor programming, and we ask our beloved helpers to begin the procedure now.

2. We ask the Beloved Blue Angels with the Blazing Blue Swords to initiate the Dogma Buster Procedure now.

3. We call upon Beloved Guido of the Light and his team of angels to remove all the curses on all layers of the programming, and replace them with love and light for the totality of _____ beingness, including all parallel and dimensional selves.

4. We say, "Ho O Pono Pono, Ho O Pono Pono, Ho O Pono Pono," for the co-creation of the programs and all negative effects of the program.

5. We call for team 1 and team 2 of the beloved Lavender Angels to initiate the identification and collection process.

6. We call for beloved Archangel Amethyst and her legions of Violet Flame Angels to transmute all etheric residuals of negative energy: from the programs, from each layer of the programming, and from the negative dendrite clearings, for

the totality of _____ beingness, including all parallel and dimensional selves.

7. We ask Beloved Mother Sekhmet if all programming connected to the identified issues are completed.

8. We say, "Ho O Pono Pono, Ho O Pono Pono, Ho O Pono Pono," and we express our love and gratitude to all the Beloveds connected to this healing.

Chapter 4

Master Stem Remnants

The master stem remnant was created to be a last line of defense against a negative program that is active and in place. There are many negative programs, and you or your client could have picked them up in any lifetime, in any dimension or parallel reality. We initiate a clearing for the master stem remnant to be activated when the person has done clearings for a particular program is experiencing the negative effects of that program, because something is still triggering its effects.

The master stem remnant is like a hidden wire that brings us back to the program that was being replicated and activates it again. When we become aware that we haven't quite completed clearing that particular program, and something still remains to be done to clear it once and for all, we can call back whatever part of the program that is needed to get the information we need to clear it. It is as if we are recalling it from associative memory, using a trigger to bring it up.

The master stem remnant is a backup; by going in and recalling it, instead of enabling the handlers to use it to control us, it will serve us because the individual will now control the memory and clearing of it. We know the purpose of having negative programs, disruptor energy, or negative entities is to ultimately clear it, so we are more grounded in the knowing we are one with Creator-Source. In doing so we allow ourselves to become aware of the experience we had with it, and we perceive the gifts we have received from it. This will bring us back into the light of love and help us remember who we are.

When we call up the master stem remnant of a negative program (disrupters and negative entities can also be thought of as negative programs, because the handlers have to pave the way for them), we empower ourselves because we are taking responsibility for having co-created it. When we clear it, not only do we do it for ourselves, but it raises the level of the vibration for the All That Is.

When the master stem remnant is still active, we feel the lingering effects of the program we have cleared and are prevented from going forward fully. It is necessary to find out what we are still holding onto that's causing the program to be active within us. There was something we didn't quite get, or else we wouldn't still be feeling the effects of the negative program.

When you clear the handlers, who are the controllers that instituted the program, you blaze the trail. Going into the negative program again to clear out the last remnant of it won't bother you as much, because the handlers have been cleared and won't be there to push your buttons as they did when you first cleared the program. Now you basically know what you're dealing with, so you're going to have a new outlook. You are more detached and are less likely to be dragged into the tar pit of your lower vibrational emotions.

You come into clearing the master stem remnant, which you can think as the last piece of the puzzle you need in order to clear the program once for all and empower yourself, as an independent and sovereign being. This will give you a different perspective of what the program is and how it affected you. You realize that in choosing to resolve it, you are looking at it as a compassionate observer who will re-experience it again just long enough to do what you need to in order to bring it to completion. Bringing up the master stem remnant in this way gives you an opportunity to have an overview of it that you didn't have before. There could be some new insight that comes to you while you are observing the replaying of that part of the program the master stem remnant is bringing up.

When you first cleared the program, you put the negative program outside of yourself by clearing the replicator, but you need to get back to observe the program just long enough to be sure of what is going on with it to see whatever is hanging around that hasn't been cleared yet. I ask you to consider the analogy of a football team. There is the first team, or what is called the starting team. All of a sudden the first team and the coaches are disabled, so the second team needs to come in.

Now you need to have someone do the coaching. Instead of playing the game against the opposition, you are playing against the master stem remnant. When you call in this second team, you can make the team more powerful now because each person on the second team is united in the function of being the coach. In order to clear the master stem remnant effectively, the individual has to see what their purpose was in creating it. Then they can choose to empower themselves and uncreate it. They have to see that they are the coach and choose to observe the master stem remnant, discern what they are still holding onto, and then clear it completely for good.

We are the interface between ourselves (or our client) and the energy behind the negative program, which can be from a disrupter residue or a negative entity. When we do the master stem remnant clearing, we call in the highest team, the highest level of health, and we infuse the remnant that appeared with a new higher program of life. In this higher program the sovereignty of the individual is honored and revered.

The individual allows himself to evolve into taking control of his own energy field. He realizes he calls the shots and creates his own reality with the power of intent. The individual owns his creation and takes the responsibility to initiate the clearing by taking out the last remnant of the negative program, whether it was based in the disruptor energy, negative entities, replicators, or individual negative dendrites. The individual realizes that the practitioner is not doing the removal for him. The individual realizes he is co-creating the removal with the practitioner and the unseen beings of love and light.

The understanding is that the clearing is going on in the higher dimensions of our being. You can think of DNA as an interdimensional filament that taps into higher levels of being. It is from this place that the program anchors itself into the four bodies of our being, and it is from this place that we clear it.

The way we get into the DNA is through our connection in our heart center and our pineal gland. This balance between the mind and heart is the connection that allows us to go within the cells and subatomic particles of our being. It is here we connect with the DNA and access the memory banks. Only the master stem remnant has remained, and now with the pure, focused intent of the person, she can look at what the remnant still holds and the message it has for her. In this way she may see the bigger picture of what her experience of having played through this program has meant, not only for herself but for the All That Is.

After people make the connection with what the master stem remnant had been holding back from the program they had cleared, it is time for them to voice their intent to clear this last piece of the puzzle, which will free them. In doing so they are empowering and liberating themselves from outside influences to control them.

Up in the higher dimensions the timelines, parallel universes, and different aspects of our being come together, it is possible to access the bigger story of why we played through any programs and even why we held onto the negative program and then cleared the master stem remnant of it.

The Master Stem Remnant Clearing

I bring in the loving energy of Lord Arcturus, the Blue Angels with Archangel Michael and the blazing blue swords of truth. I bring in the loving inspirational energies of the Lavender Angels and Arch Angel Amethyst. I bring forth beloved Meg Hoopes.

This is one last opportunity to recall this negative program if you wish to do so. Do you want to clear the master stem remnant out now, so that it is no more? Do you own the creation of the part you played in experiencing this negative program? Do you forgive yourself for all the pain and separation you felt while experiencing it? Let us go ahead and clear this master stem remnant.

I call forth Mother Sekhmet. We put out our intent to bring up the master stem remnant. Mother Sekhmet uses her hand like a wand with gold and platinum light radiating forth. Her wand brings up the negative program. The motion of her hand creates a spiral effect that allows us to sift through the program in linear time. We are searching for the message of what has been held back from us in clearing this program. It may be revealed through our senses, or it may come to us on a wave of light, a download of information, or in some other way.

We are examining our feelings as we settle upon one specific moment in time that contains the master stem remnant. It is here that we hear, see, or feel a playback of a moment in time when the replicator and the negative program took root. This brings up the thoughts and emotions we were going through, which are the essence of the negative program.

We ask that any information that is still active within the negative program be revealed to us at this time by any means possible. It is within this core moment of the negative program that we bless, praise, and respect the feeling of fear that permeates this scene.

We say, "I choose not to live under the dominance of the wheel of fear. I choose to be free, to live and express my life as the divine, galactic being I Am. I choose to clear the master stem remnant as the last remnant of this program, in any and all dimensions and parallel realities." And so it is.

We ask for any further information about the purpose and meaning of our experience of this program to be imparted to us either consciously or subconsciously in our dream state.

We give praise, gratitude, respect, and love to all the beings who helped us with this clearing.

Chapter 5

Information about Disrupter Removal

by Meg Hoopes

The Disrupter Story

Meg started clearing disrupters a relatively short time before she died. I feel it is important to give you some background on disrupters, the evolution of the disrupter clearings, and how any of the disrupter energy that is still left is now cleared in the negative program clearings.

For a year or two before she passed away, Meg led what she called a Whammy Group comprised of some of her friends and teachers of the spirited clearings.

A December 2009 Update from Meg on the Completion of Disruptor Removals:

At the time the Whammy Group worked on this, we were 93 percent effective in removing the disrupters for the planet. After that Whammy Group exercise, I worked with removing a few disruptors that were blocked from us. One of my clients had a disrupter, and I asked if it was timely to remove the rest of the disrupters from humanity and got a yes.

When I did these clearings, the team was composed of the Blue Angels with their blazing blue swords, the Z'Or Continuum angels, medical teams from the ships, and the Violet Flame Angels. I believe Sekmet, Ashtar, and still others oversaw our project. I instructed the blue angels to use their magical swords to find those with the disrupter protected by the shell placed around it. An angel was assigned to each person with the disrupter. The angels were instructed to shape shift the blue sword into a laser gun with a sight. They found the seam of the protective casing and opened it with the laser. A Z'Or Continuum angel immediately scrambled the program of the disrupter and converted it to a normal microbiological cell compatible to the human body.

The medical teams from the Galactic ships swept in and removed the casing and transmuted it to neutral energy, sending it to the void. The Violet Flame Angels came in and transmuted all residual energies and also blessed and cleared each human body. I asked for a report on the effectiveness of what was done and got 98 percent. And so it is.

An important learning experience for me during the last several years is that if I want information, I must intend to receive it. Curiosity, caring, discussion, and study are not enough; I must intend to receive the information and know that I will ask the right questions and receive truth in the answers. When I prepare to receive information by getting into a meditative state, I do so knowing that I will know what questions to ask. This usually takes the form of me describing what has me curious and that I want answers and information about how the process works.

I ask for assistance from my Mighty I AM Presence, my Guides and Guardian Angels, Ascended Masters, Ascended Lady Masters, Archangels and any Cosmic Being who may have information for me. Then I ask and expect to access my illumined mind. I use muscle response testing to validate my illumined knowingness and the completeness of the instructions and information I am receiving. Then in a state of gratitude I apply the information for myself and others. As I recognize the pattern and ask more questions that need answers, I am always given the answers.

I will now describe my experience of learning about disrupters and how to nullify their effects.

I awoke at three in the morning and could not go back to sleep. I got out of bed and moved to my recliner chair in the front room. "What is keeping me awake and making me so restless?" I wondered. I went into a meditative state and began to make statements of my concerns, asking for guidance. I focused on the many e-mails and reports on the Internet describing the attempts and failures to break free from national and global dominance of the Illuminati families. I asked, "Is there something I can do to help remove the blockages?"

Three years ago I had been given information and instruction on how to remove the chip placed by the Illuminati scientists in humans; the chips were programmed to go off when they were activated. I wondered if there was something else contributing to the present situation. I was told there was a device called a disrupter designed to disrupt harmony, peace, and balance in humans, families, and organizations.

I asked to be shown what this device was and who created it. The disrupter is a microscopic, biological implant designed originally by the Annunaki and refined and maintained by the Illuminati scientists. It was placed in humans as a control mechanism to ensure slavery and compliance. Once placed in a human, it is passed through the blood lines.

It has a sensor that is activated when we are in a negative environment by anything that is not of the love frequency. A switch that is part of the sensor has three settings: neutral, forward, and reverse. I was shown by my spirit what this looked like; it was magnified in size until I could see it. I was told that I knew how to neutralize it and nullify its effects.

The removal that originally was used was very detailed in explaining to the angels how the disrupter needed to be cleared. This is no longer needed because the guidance we use for the clearings, such as Arch Angel

Amethyst & the Violet Flame Angels, are entrained to the procedure. All that is necessary is for us to give our pure intent, and it is done in their rhythm and timing.

The clearing of the disrupter has evolved to such a level that now when we clear disrupter energy, we do so while doing the negative program removals.

Chapter 6

Living in Your Compassionate Heart
by Meg Hoopes

Preparation

Clear your aura. Check for and remove handlers. Ask for your team to be in attendance. Clear the space and ask for protection for everyone. Ask for Mother Sekhmet and your Guardian Angels to be on alert. Call for the White Light to surround each individual and the space.

Introduction

Your Compassionate Heart is in the top part of your heart chakra. In it is the energy of pure unconditional Love. It is here that your spirit, your soul lives. The more you live here, the more information you receive from your illumined mind. It is here that you get confirmation of truth.

To live in our Compassionate Hearts and complete the ascension, we need essential parts to be in the Compassionate Heart. Two of these are the ego and the inner child.

"Along with feeling of separation comes a tug of war. Are you going to be guided by the ego or the inner child? Who is going to rule in this instant? By bringing them into your heart space, you are preparing the ego for ascension with you, because you cannot leave the ego behind and be a completely ascended being. You need to bring the ego with you, but you need to put the ego into an atmosphere of love. Don't leave out your parallel and dimensional selves."3*

The ego sees itself as your protector. The instant your energy drops to 3-D i.e. duality, the ego is out there to protect you.

Procedures

1. Imagine your heart center as one of divine love. One of its inhabitants is a loving angel with the attributes of both mother and father. It has a big lap and loving arms made for cuddling. Give your ego and your inner child a name. Call them by name, send them loving energy, and ask them to join you by sitting in the lap of the angel. Tell them how much you love them and appreciate the service they provide you. Assure them that you are not complete without them. Let's have a parts party. Invite the following to join the party in your compassionate heart: your inner teenager, your inner young adult, and as appropriate, your inner adult self, your inner senior self, your mother or father self, your grandmother or grandfather self, and any other parts that you think are relevant. Invite in your other lifetimes and their many parts. Your compassionate heart has an unlimited capacity for all lives and all parts. Love each life, each part and sing them a song of love, blessings, and gratitude. Feel the fullness and the splendor of your compassionate love and the oneness of all that you are. I AM THAT I AM!

2. David Roth wrote the words and the music for this song. Meg used to play it on the calls when we were doing the compassionate heart exercise.

Will You Come Home © David Roth

www.davidrothmusic.com

used by permission

I know where you live, but you've never been home

Everyone in your house has been living alone

Now something is wrong and you know it's not fair

But it's easier to hide than to show that you care

CHORUS

Will you come home, will you come home

Will you come home to your heart

You've kept away from yourself from the start

But you can come home now, come home to your heart

You work hard all day, how you strain to stand tall

Trying to make someone love you, better yet make them all

But the doors have been closed, all your secrets concealed

And you're living your life so they're never revealed

CHORUS

Leave the baggage behind, you've done more than your part

Before you fill all your loved ones you must fill your own heart

Don't look to others for directions or deeds

You're the very first love that your heart ever needs

CHORUS

You've kept away from yourself from the start

But you can come home now

Come home to your heart

3.   Now surrounded by love and joined with your parts, I am going to take you on a guided trip. Prepare to have a good time.

The Compassionate Heart Exercise

With your hand over your heart, I want you to breathe deeply and consciously, and I'll count to seven. When we get to seven, we'll be there, and I'll describe where we are. One, two, three, four, five, six, seven.

Now keep your eyes closed and see with your inside eyes as I explain and describe what a wonderful place we are in. We're at the top of the mountains in a meadow. The mountain meadow is filled with wildflowers and bees and butterflies and unicorns and elves, and it's a very busy little place. The grass is so lush and so soft, and you move out there with your party, your parts party, and everybody wants to take part in this. And so they do, and each one of them lies down on the grass. As you lie down on the grass, you can feel the love in your heart center moving down your back and going down into the earth, and it meets the compassionate love coming from the earth, and you join together in harmony and in peace.

Now as you lie down on the grass, everybody gets close to each other so that they can reach out and touch a leg or a foot. We have tiny children out there, little babes who want to lie on the grass. They don't want to be held, but they want to lie on the grass. Little children, the inner child, the ego, the teenager, the old crones, the magicians—they're all there, and they're all touching, and everybody has put their heads on somebody's belly.

Now we have this intricate connection, with everybody feeling everyone's compassionate love, and suddenly somebody starts to giggle—it's a child. Then somebody else starts to laugh, and pretty soon everybody's laughing, everybody's stomach is jumping and they're just having the best time, and it's so lovely now. Laughter heals, so laugh. Wherever you are, laugh out loud and feel the loving harmony of Mother Earth, feel yourself joining your compassionate heart with hers and send her your gratitude and your blessings, telling her how much you enjoy living with her and on her and how much you enjoy serving her with these clearings.

Now I'm going to count to seven, and when we reach seven, you'll be back in your space. One, two, three . . . take that smile with you. Four, five, six, seven. And there you are, filled with love and totally connected to Mother Gaia and all of your parts. Just enjoy who you are, the majesty of who you are.

Chapter 7

Present Life Cleanse

This activity is about cleansing, purifying, and beautifying your present life. Many persons and incidents in our lives remain in our memory, stored in the cells of our bodies as well as in our brains. Although these incidents and people are rarely thought about, and we may never see them anymore, there are faint—or in some cases, strong—streams of energy connecting us to them.

Thought forms of varying strength are attached to them and maintain the connections. This includes family stories told over and over again through the years. Many of these incidents are attached to a traumatic experience for that time in your life. As an accumulation, they form a drag on us, focusing some of our attention and energy on the past. Have you found yourself suddenly remembering an incident from the past that seems to have no bearing on what you are doing or who you are presently? You gained the wisdom from the experience and do not need to have energy attached to the persons or incident. In fact, that energy freed can be used in your present.

This activity is not a lobotomy exercise. You may still have the memory, but it will have no power to disrupt you in the Now moment. You will find many examples of what I have described as you do this activity.

It may take hours or even days to complete; you may come back to it each month, cleaning the past month or week or day. I divided my life in six-year increments, doing one increment a day or every few days. Then I realized doing it that soon was too fast for my body, so I listened to inner guidance as to how soon I could do the increments. Sometimes I go directly to an incident and speak about it, highlighting smell, taste, touch, hearing, sight, emotions, and thoughts. Be the observer; don't get caught in the story. There are many ways to do this present life cleanse. Be alert to a need to insert a fear release where needed.

Outline for the Activity

1. Do a general fear release about doing this activity. You may have already experienced some fear in reading the introduction.

2. Set aside some uninterrupted time for this activity; you need not do it all at once. Make a list of time frames, incidents, geographic locations, et cetera, in order to focus the cleanse. For example: the time from conception to birth, and the first six years of your life and all incidents and relationships during that time; a time of serious illness, yours or someone close to you; school in all its increments; extended family activities. Or you can begin now and work back in time. For example, select the time frame of now through the last six years. Listen to your inner guidance. If fears come up while you are doing this list, do a fear release. I use a time frame in my examples, but remember you can cleanse an incident, all interaction with specific people, and more.

3. Identify and speak out loud the time frame, specific incident, or however you have identified what you want to cleanse. Review the details that come up for you. Do not spend a lot of time on details; just acknowledge them.

This is an inclusive cleanse that will cut the attachments to that which you remember and that which you do not remember. You will find that you also acknowledge the positive parts of whatever you are cleansing.

4. Now call to the angels.

    "Mighty I AM Presence I call in the Legions of Angels with the Limitless Sacred Fire Power to cleanse and purify _____ (fill in what you want) from my present life. Consume all discordant energy streams from me to incidents, conditions, people, places, and things. In particular, I ask that you cleanse and purify attachments formed through the five physical senses: sight, smell, hearing, taste, and touch, both conscious and unconscious. I call back all aspects of myself splintered off and given to incidents, persons, places, conditions, and things. I love, honor, praise, and thank you for your assistance, the legions of angels with the limitless sacred fire power."

    Remain quiet. Allow them time to do this service and your body time to adjust.

5. It is now time to beautify and bless the time frame or incident in your life that has been cleansed and purified.

    "In gratitude I call forth all ascended beings and energies, including the angelic hosts, connected to the Office of the Christ and the Christ within. Send forth your energies of aqua and fuchsia colors to bathe, bless, and beautify the time frame in my life. I call forth the fragrance of roses, the Music of the Spheres, angel breath on my face, the taste of a delicate golden ambrosia in my mouth, and soft pink and silver light touching and bathing my eyes. Bless my bodies with Herculean strength, wisdom, peace, harmony, grace, victory, purity, and love."

6. You can add anything you want to this present time cleanse and beautification. Remember to bless and thank all blessed beings who are assisting you. Also acknowledge yourself for your diligence and love of self in doing this activity.

CHAPTER 8

Bringing It All Home

Spirited Clearings is meant as a way for each of us to accelerate our ascension process. A key component of Spirited Clearings is trusting in our intuition on this path of remembering that we are all divine beings derived from the same source. We do this when we take back our power by removing the negative programming and transmuting this energy into high frequencies of love and light.

I have presented the language of Meg's contributions, and mine, to these clearings. Meg originated the clearings in the spirit of non-attachment and experimentation. We recognize that the light continues to dominate the energy of our planet. Spirited Clearings are always evolving and the language we have used is not meant to be finite. What we have presented is a viable assortment of techniques for everyone to begin taking back the power that we have given to the dark forces that created this negative programming.

We encourage those of you who incorporate Spirited Clearings into your own work to use your guidance for adapting these teachings for the benefit of all, including Mother Gaia.

Validating the information we receive by way of MRT, or using a pendulum, is an effective way to implement the wisdom of Spirited

Clearings. When we go to the originating lifetime of a negative program we are using it as a starting point in clearing all programming associated with it. To me the language of these clearings is a testament to Meg's perseverance and to the connection she had with her guidance team.

The different versions of the clearings that Meg left behind have shown me the evolution of her work in conjunction with the rising consciousness levels in this period of time. The changes in the wording of the clearings recognize the concept that our angels and guides became entrained with our intents, so we no longer needed to go into much detail about how the clearings were being done.

I have come to interpret the part that Meg played in releasing Spirited Clearings as someone who is providing people, who are waking up to their purpose in being here, with viable ways to bridge the duality of the 3rd dimension to the state of full consciousness in the 5th dimension and beyond.

Ultimately being the love that we all are is the reason for us being here; this means being a master at learning to love ourselves for who we are and the part we are playing in manifesting the godhead while creating within this hologram. We cannot be love as long we are in anyway holding onto fear based programming; to remove and transmute the energy of the lower vibrations into high frequencies of love & light is our purpose in presenting Spirited Clearings.

Appendices

Appendix A

Dogma Buster

Whammy Group

July 26, 2009

Our lives have been guided by dogmas, beliefs, and experiences taught by others as truths. We were expected to accept them as our truths, and we often did. Those who questioned the truth of the dogmas or wanted more information about their source were scorned, killed, ridiculed, and ignored. In politics, corporations, religions, families, organizations, education, and everywhere there are human exchanges, there are dogmas that ignore personal rights of the individual. We are living·in a time of housecleaning, in preparation for receiving and being our full consciousness while still in human bodies. Dogmas are untruths. Therefore, it is time for a Dogma Buster clearing.

Dogma Buster Clearing of Evil Teaching and Practices

Names often used by groups and individuals in rites, ceremonies, and worship.

Names of the Negative Deity: Lucifer, Satan, Devil, the Lord of the Dark, Bringer of the Light, Raphmore, Loky, Beast, Hecate, Beelzeba

Satan worshipers: black witches, black warlords

Activities: Drinking human blood sacrifices, blood and urine of young sacrificed goats; black candles, altars; dancing nude, sexual perversions, gang power by sexually using young women tied to the altar; killing as part of ritual, killing as punishment for breaking the Devil's laws; oaths and rituals for joining a group or individual worship; secrecy; giving the mark of Satan as part of ritual; robbing a child's grave to use the dirt in ritual; wearing black robes and masks; using whores as sacrifices; fanatical beliefs.

We are listing these activities, because this dark energy is kept in secret from the masses by the controlling elite. These practices are the underlying dynamics of the agenda they have carried on, from the times of Atlantis to the present, which the Annunaki passed onto them. Their dogmas form the rationale of the institutions they have used to make themselves the Controllers, Observers, and Protectors of society.

Dogma buster clearings are now part of the negative program removals. They are an important part of dismantling the matrices of negative programming. We do a forgiveness and mercy piece for all participants, including ourselves. Dendrite removal is part of the negative program removals. All judgments, condemnations, and explorations used to connect dendrites to the negative programs are cleared.

Appendix B

A Story from Meg about Clearing a Past Lifetime, 1/23/10

Today I was contemplating that I did not as yet have a spiritual understanding of what my current physical conditions were about. Not receiving any information, I picked up a book I was reading: *"Shakkai: The Women in the Garden"* by Lynn V. Andrews.

As I read a description of Lynn floating out in the universe, the thought came that I was not free to do that because I was bound to my four-body system in some way. I became aware of a binding around my physical body that covered the distance between my second and third charka and was very tight. I gained more water, which bloated me, and the binding became tighter.

The first question I asked was, "Is this about another lifetime I am to clear?" I got yes. I asked to have that lifetime revealed to me. I was an apprentice to a very powerful witch; I was recruited and felt very special. However, the more I got into the craft, the less I wanted to be a witch. I ran away several times but was always brought back. The witch told me I could not escape her. She weaved this strong band and placed it around me with a tether attached to me and to her. All she had to do was pull on the tether, and it tightened.

That was all I was shown of that lifetime, but I was very aware of the band. I asked if negative dendrite removal would remove the band. Yes. I set up my teams. There were many, many curses put on me. My lavender angels called in twelve more angels. The identification and collection process took a long time, and it took even more time to clear curses. When the removal and transmutation to love energy started, it also took a long time. As this went on, I was breathing much easier, with some of the cramping moved out of my stomach. When we were finished I said I could still feel the band. I was told I was feeling the bloat. I asked if this clearing completed the clearing for that lifetime. Yes.

Appendix C

Your Chakras

The other things that shift function are your chakra systems. You have a total of fourteen major chakras that exist multi-dimensionally—seven within your physical body, seven outside your body—plus the alpha and omega chakras. Most people see or feel chakras as radiant, spinning energy sources, but chakras also have a sixth-dimensional internal structure.

Under the karma game, the structure of the seven embodied chakras was deliberately limited so that they could only transduce energy from the astral plane; they were "sealed." With this limited blueprint, a chakra looks like two cones. One of the cones opens out toward the front of the body; the other one opens out toward the back. Where their narrowed points touch in the center of the body, they are sealed so that they remain in this configuration. This narrow part in the center tends to be clogged with mental and emotional debris, causing the spin of the cones to slow down or stop, which starves the acupuncture meridian system of energy and can cause illness or death. This type of chakra structure can only move energy front to back or back to front and cannot utilize higher-dimensional frequencies.

During our time of ascension we prepare ourselves for the shift from the third dimension to the fifth dimension, the density of our physical body rises up in vibration, so that we can become filled with light. When the lightbody process is activated, the seals in the center points are broken, and the chakra structure gradually opens up from the center until the chakra is spherical in shape. This allows the chakra to radiate energy in all directions and begin to transduce frequencies from the higher dimensions. The body sheds the collected karmic debris, and the spherical blueprint makes it impossible for any more to collect. The spheres keep expanding in size, until all the chakras merge as one unified energy field.

Each of the upper chakras (the non-embodied chakras) have a different geometric blueprint structure, one that is appropriate for transducing the specific dimensional or Oversoul frequencies associated with the chakra. The eighth and eleventh chakras also contain flat, crystalline templates through which the galactic axiotonal lines pass. Once one's axiotonal meridians are reconnected, the Oversoul uses these templates to modulate the star influences on one's physical body. The Oversoul recalibrates the axiotonal lines and the axial circulatory system through the eighth chakra. Therefore, the eighth chakra acts as the master control for the mutation of the body's systems and the merging of the energy bodies.

Until recently, the alpha and omega "chakras" have been vestigial in the human body type. Even though they are energy centers, they have a completely different type of blueprint and function than that of the other chakras. They are finely tuned energy regulators for electric, magnetic, and gravitational waves, as well as serving as anchors for the seventh-dimensional, etheric blueprint.

The alpha chakra is six to eight inches above and about two inches forward from the center of your head. It connects you to your immortal body of light in the fifth dimension. The omega chakra is about eight inches below the end of your spine and connects you to the planet as a hologram, as well as to your entire holographic grid of incarnations. Unlike the fourth-dimensional karmic matrix, this is a completely non-karmic type of connection. The eighth chakra is seven to nine inches above the exact center of the head, above the alpha chakra. There is a column of light, about four inches in diameter that extends from your eighth chakra down through the center of your body, through the embodied chakras and to about eight inches below your feet. This column supports a tube of light, about one and three-quarters inches in diameter, which runs down the exact center of the entire length of the column.

When the alpha and omega chakras are open and operating correctly, you will experience something called the waves of Metatron moving through the inner column of light. These magnetic, electric, and gravitational waves oscillate back and forth between the alpha and omega chakras, which regulate the waves' amplitude and frequency. These waves stimulate and support the flow of pranic life force energy in the smaller tube of light. The waves of Metatron also assist in coordinating the physical body's mutation to the preexisting template of your immortal body of light.

As the embodied chakras open into their spherical structure, grids are laid down that connect the chakras directly into spin points on the skin's surface, thereby connecting the chakras directly into the new axiotonal and axial systems. By connecting the chakra grids into the axiotonal lines, the chakras are hooked up into higher evolutionary, universal resonance grids and wave motions that assist the chakras and the emotional, mental, and spiritual bodies to merge into one unified energy field. This unified field then receives the Oversoul bodies and moves in synch with universal waves and pulses. This whole new system then transmits these waves and pulses through the spin points into the axial circulatory system, to recalibrate the pulses and flows of bodily fluids.

Now, in a karma game, because there is the perception you are in a state of separation from spirit and living in a state of limitation, and you're alienated from your physical body, that usually means that you're not in your body. If you are not in your body, you cannot activate the heart chakra.

If you cannot activate your heart chakra, the chakras that are operating predominantly are the base chakra, the navel chakra, and the solar plexus chakra; all of your interactions are coming out of instinctive terror, karmic patterning, power, lust, greed, or sheer ego-centered power interactions with people. You don't get to have a higher interaction until you are fully in your body—and of course, until then the upper, non-embodied chakras are not activated at all.

The pineal gland plays an important role along with the heart when we use our power of intent to tune into the higher frequencies that are being beamed to us in this time of shift to full consciousness. When the pineal gland and the heart center are balanced and working in harmony with one another, we are able to process these light encodings to accelerate our ascension process.

Appendix D

The Dimensions

First, let me briefly describe the various dimensions or planes of existence in our model. We use a twelve-dimensional model, and you, sitting here in a physical body, exist in the third dimension; it's matter based. The fourth dimension is what's called the astral plane; it's mainly emotionally based. Together, these two make up what we call the lower creation world. These are the dimensions where the game of separation is carried out. These are the only dimensions in which the illusion of good and evil can be maintained and in which you can feel separated from spirit and from each other. You've all become quite good at doing that, and it's been a very successful game of separation, but now it's time for it to end. This planet is in a state of ascension and is currently vibrating at the lower levels of the astral plane. As part of the ascension process, all of the dimensions will be rolled up into the higher dimensions and will cease to exist.

Because the planet is now vibrating at the level of the mid-astral plane, it's beginning to feel like a dream state for many people, who are never quite sure if they are awake or asleep. Continuities are breaking down. There is the feeling that things can change as you hold them in your hand. The pen that you're writing with may become a hammer, and eventually this lack of continuity will no longer bother you, just as it doesn't when you're dreaming. You'll be noticing that your dream states are changing, that as you wake up you're not quite sure if you're awake. You will become lucid while you're dreaming, fully conscious in that state. You will be self-aware as you move back and forth between different realities, and all of them will feel equally real to you. It won't seem like there is only one true reality anymore.

The fifth through the ninth dimensions make up the mid-creation realm. The fifth is the lightbody dimension, in which you are aware of yourself as a master and a multidimensional being. In the fifth dimension, you are completely spiritually oriented. Many of you have come in from this plane to be light workers here.

The sixth dimension holds the templates for the DNA patterns of all types of species' creation—including humankind. It's also where the light languages are stored, and it is made up mostly of color and tone. It is the dimension where consciousness creates through thought and one of the places where you work during sleep. It can be difficult to get a bead on this, because you're not in a body unless you choose to create one. When you are operating sixth-dimensionally, you are more of an alive thought; you create through your consciousness, but you don't necessarily have a vehicle for that consciousness.

The seventh dimension is that of pure creativity, pure light, pure tone, pure geometry, and pure expression. It is a plane of infinite refinement and the last plane where you perceive yourself as an individual.

The eighth is the dimension of the group mind or group soul and this is where your world touches base with the vaster part of who you are. It is characterized by the loss of a sense of "I." When you travel multi-dimensionally, this is the plane where you would have the most trouble keeping your consciousness together, because you are pure "we," operating with group goals, so it might seem as though you've gone to sleep or blanked out.

In the model that we use, the ninth dimension is the plane of the collective consciousness of planets, star systems, galaxies, and dimensions. If you visit this dimension, it can be difficult to remain conscious. Once again, it's very difficult to get a sense of "I," because you are so vast that everything is you. Imagine being the consciousness of a galaxy! Every life form, star, planet, and group mind in it is within you.

The tenth through twelfth dimensions make up the upper creation realm. The tenth is the source of the rays, home of what are called the Elohim. This is where new plans of creation are designed and then sent into the mid-creation levels. You can have a sense of "I" at this level, but it won't be at all what you're used to at the third dimension.

The eleventh dimension is that of preformed light—the point before creation and a state of exquisite expectancy, just like the moment before a sneeze or an orgasm. It is the realm of the being known as Metatron, and of archangels and other Akashics for the source-system. There are planetary Akashic records and galactic Akashics, as well as the Akashic for an entire source-system. You are in one source-system of many. If you go to another source-system, what you will experience will be different.

The twelfth dimension is the one point where all consciousness knows itself to be utterly one with All That Is. There is *no* separation of any kind. If you tap into this level, you know yourself to be completely one with All That Is, with the creator force. If you tap in there, you will never be the same again, because you cannot sustain the same degree of separation if you have experienced complete unity.

Appendix E

Glossary of Terms and Beings

Archangel Amethyst: She uses the violet flame ray, from the flowers of passionate resolve, to disassemble the blockages that we build around the heart. She shines universal love and light to transmute all of the lower vibrations into the highest frequencies of love and light with the help of her Violet Flame angels.

Archangel Charity: Teaches us that giving and receiving are different parts of the same energy exchange, and that we have nothing to fear in giving when we are touched in our hearts to do so. We are unlimited in our abundance and our capacity to spread joy, love, and warmth.

Archangel Faith: Teaches us steadfastness, to stick to our plan, to be unwavering, to know we have the support of the universes, and that we are worthy of receiving our most ardent desires.

Archangel Hope: Teaches us to imagine our wildest dreams and then to have the courage to know that they have already been given to us in the moment we ask for them.

Archangel Michael: Associated with the blue sword of truth, sometimes called Excalibur.

Ego: This is the third-dimensional part of you that protects you. It needs to be kept in balance, and one of the most beneficial ways you can do this is to raise the level of your vibration on a constant basis. You can always tell the ego that you are safe and appreciate all it has done in helping you get this far on your journey.

Guido of the Light: A master builder, a carpenter, a practitioner of Feng Shui. He makes sure the light finds its way into your heart. He removes the barriers and obstacles of the physical to ensure that the light penetrates your heart. You can think of Guido as the foremen, and his angels are his building crew. It's as if your heart is the temple and the shrine of your being. He makes sure that no impurities prevent the light and love from coming in and taking their place on the throne of your heart.

Inner Child: Your inner child is the part of you that is pure and innocent. This aspect of your being may have split off the timeline with you at an early age. It is helpful to align yourself with the energy of the inner child, and in this way you are healing your own timeline.

Mother Mary: She is the mother of Sananda in her incarnation of Earth, and she is one of the Kumaras. She brings the roses of the Kumaras to us, which are a symbol of unconditional, universal love.

Ramtha

Meg attended Ramtha's School of Enlightenment. The name Ramtha is claimed to be derived from *Ram* and to mean "the God" in Ramtha's language. He is an entity whom J. Z. Knight claims to channel. According to Ramtha, he was a Lemurian warrior who fought the Atlanteans over 35,000 years ago. Knight became his first student of what he calls the great work.

The St Germaine "I Am" Sanctuary

Guy W. Ballard founded the sanctuary and published his first book in 1934 under the name of Godfre Ray King. Out of the discourse by the ascended masters, Mr. and Mrs. Ballard founded the "I Am" Activity under the daily direction of Saint Germain. The parent organization is Saint Germain Foundation, with worldwide headquarters located in Schaumburg, Illinois, a suburb of Chicago. It is represented throughout the world by three hundred local groups termed "I Am" Sanctuary, "I Am" Temple, "I Am" Study Groups, or "I Am" Reading Room.

Appendix F

Contact List

http://www.spiritedclearings.com/index.html

These practitioners have continued on with Meg's work. They are ready, willing, and able to help you with integrating Meg's spirited clearings into your ascension journey.

Katharina Waldorf

    katwald@prodigy.net.mx

    Waldorf.Katharina@gmail.com

    http://www.spiritedclearings.com/practitioners.html

Eli Galla

    eli@oholful.com

    http://oholful.com

    http://www.spiritedclearings.com/practitioners.html

FOOTNOTES

1. Lifespring was founded in 1974 by John Hanley and four others, though by 1978 he was the president and sole remaining founder, essentially leading the work himself with the support of his wife, Candace, who worked with him throughout the many years of Lifespring's extensive work. Presently, his son, John Hanley, Jr., is working together with John Hanley Sr. to pioneer the field of experiential education in Corporate America through their company, Leadership Training and Development Group (LTDG).

2. James Oliver Cyr, M.D.—The Spiritual Hierarchy-The Elders of The Race, The Spiritual Government, and The Great White Brotherhood (white referring to The Light that they radiate). There are seven great Divisions within The Hierarchy, each working with the vast energies of one of The Seven Rays to influence planetary affairs, and each Division is headed by one of The Lords or Chohans of The Seven Rays. (These are human designations only—for easier comprehension.)

   At the head of this Hierarchy is The One Who is called Sanat Kumara. This Being may rightly be considered as The Lord of the World and has also been referred to as "The One Initiator", "The Youth of Endless Summers", and "The Ancient of Days" in The Bible.

3. Ashtar channeled through Susan Leland:
   http://www.spiritedclearings.com/egoinnerchild.html